Digital Social Entrepreneurship

This book discusses the emerging phenomenon of digital social entrepreneurship, which relies on the use and embracement of new technologies, and investigates the social implications and value for people, profit, and planet.

The authors examine the use of new technologies such as artificial intelligence, metaverse, and augmented reality to understand the evolution of social entrepreneurialism, considering three layers: micro, meso, and macro. The micro layer analyses digital social entrepreneurs' attitude in generating new digital social innovation for disadvantaged people; the meso layer explores the combination of digital and social initiatives in an entrepreneurial journey to improve inclusiveness and sustainability; and the macro layer investigates the impact of exogenous events on Digital Social Entrepreneurship (DSE) to scaling such ventures, also offering an overview of disadvantaged entrepreneurs.

Offering new insights, research, and practical guidance, this book will appeal in particular to scholars and post graduate students of entrepreneurship and small business management, organisational studies, technology, and innovation management.

Veronica Scuotto is Associate Professor at the University of Naples Federico II after working at the University of Turin, at the Pôle Universitaire Léonard de Vinci in Paris and at the University of the West of Scotland.

Norris Krueger is Visiting Research Fellow, QREC, Kyushu University and Adjunct Professor, American University. He is a top-ranked scholar (Stanford/Elsevier top 2% list), experienced educator, and active in practitioner circles.

Manlio Del Giudice is Full Professor of Management, Head of the Department of Management and Economics, and Director of the Research Center in Data Analysis, Intelligence, Security and Information at Pegaso Digital University, Italy.

Routledge Focus on Business and Management

The fields of business and management have grown exponentially as areas of research and education. This growth presents challenges for readers trying to keep up with the latest important insights. *Routledge Focus on Business and Management* presents small books on big topics and how they intersect with the world of business research.

Individually, each title in the series provides coverage of a key academic topic, whilst collectively, the series forms a comprehensive collection across the business disciplines.

Entrepreneurship Education and Student Empowerment
Innovation in the EU
Chiara Bartoli and Federica Brunetta

Critical Thinking in Public Policy and Management
Michael Macaulay

Digital Social Entrepreneurship
Implications for People, Planet and Profit
Edited by Veronica Scuotto, Norris Krueger, and Manlio Del Giudice

AI and the Future of Leadership
Opportunities and Threats for Hybrid Organizations
Adrian Jarvis

Digital Social Entrepreneurship
Implications for People, Planet, and Profit
Edited by Veronica Scuotto, Norris Krueger, and Manlio Del Giudice

For more information about this series, please visit: www.routledge.com/Routledge-Focus-on-Business-and-Management/book-series/FBM

Digital Social Entrepreneurship

Implications for People, Planet, and Profit

Edited by Veronica Scuotto, Norris Krueger, and Manlio Del Giudice

Routledge
Taylor & Francis Group
LONDON AND NEW YORK

First published 2026
by Routledge
4 Park Square, Milton Park, Abingdon, Oxon OX14 4RN

and by Routledge
605 Third Avenue, New York, NY 10158

Routledge is an imprint of the Taylor & Francis Group, an informa business

British Library Cataloguing-in-Publication Data
A catalogue record for this book is available from the British Library

ISBN: 978-1-032-95158-4 (hbk)
ISBN: 978-1-032-95161-4 (pbk)
ISBN: 978-1-003-58344-8 (ebk)

DOI: 10.4324/9781003583448

Typeset in Times New Roman
by SPi Technologies India Pvt Ltd (Straive)

Contents

Figures

Tables

Boxes

About the Editors

Veronica Scuotto is Associate Professor at the University of Naples Federico II after working at the University of Turin, at the Pôle Universitaire Léonard de Vinci in Paris and at the University of the West of Scotland. She obtained the Italian National Qualification as full professor in 2020. She has been awarded for being a highly cited researcher by Clarivate since 2022 and by Researcher.com (2025). Her research interests are focused on entrepreneurship, social entrepreneurship, and digital technologies which have resulted in the publication of more than 90 articles featured in high ranking peer reviewed journals and books. Veronica covers a variety of editorial roles.

Norris Krueger wears many hats. As a scholar, he remains on the Stanford/Elsevier Top 2% highest impact list. Studying entrepreneurial learning and entrepreneurial ecosystems. Pioneer in social and sustainable entrepreneurship and neuroentrepreneurship. Co-organises world's biggest ecosystems research workshop. As an educator has won multiple awards for course design. Currently works with QREC (Kyushu). and American University. As a policy expert, Senior Subject Matter Expert for entrepreneurship education and ecosystems (OECD, EU, HEInnovate). As a practitioner, he serves on the ESHIP Alliance Leadership Council. Supported multiple local/regional/national initiatives. Norris is a scholar, writer, speaker, educator, relentless entrepreneurial champion and connector. Agent provocateur.

Manlio Del Giudice is Full Professor of Management, Head of the Department of Management and Economics, Director of the Research Center in Data Analysis, Intelligence, Security and Information at Pegaso Digital University. He holds the role of Editor in Chief of the *Journal of Knowledge Management* and holds top editorial positions in flagship mainstream journals in his field. Listed among the most influential scientific profiles in global research since the first edition (2020) by Stanford University and in 1st place among the Italian Full Professors in the field of Managerial, Economic and Social Sciences research. His profile boasts over 200 international publications.

Contributors

Seffusatti Alice is a PhD candidate in Management for Nonprofit Organisations at the Center for Philanthropy Studies (CEPS), Faculty of Business and Economics, University of Basel. Her research focuses on the role of Nonprofit Organisations in achieving the UN Sustainable Development Goals. She holds a double Master's degree in Economics and International Policies, an Executive Master's degree in Leadership for International Relations, and a Bachelor's degree in Business Administration.

Alan Martin is a dynamic enterprise educator and former entrepreneur and business consultant who transitioned into academia in 2019 at the University of the West of Scotland. With over 15 years of business experience, he successfully founded and managed multiple retail ventures, excelling in business planning, team building, and performance growth. His hands-on expertise now enriches his teaching of enterprise and entrepreneurship mentoring modules. Recognised for his impactful teaching during the pandemic, he has twice been nominated for Lecturer of the Year. Alan holds an MSc in International Marketing, a BA in Business (Hons), and is currently pursuing a PhD at UWS.

Dominik Meier is Assistant Professor of Global Philanthropy and Visiting Researcher at the University of Oxford. His research combines big data, machine learning and NLP to analyse individual and institutional philanthropy. He studies prosocial behaviours such as giving and volunteering, and focuses on how philanthropy can contribute to the Sustainable Development Goals (SDGs).

Dr Alan Murray is a Reader in Enterprise at the University of the West of Scotland where he is also the Enterprise Lead for the School of Business and Creative Industries and Director of the Transformative Enterprise Research Group (TERG). He has an extensive background as a business practitioner in industry and as an academic with a proven track record as a successful, innovative and award winning entrepreneur. His work as an enterprise educator has been recognised nationally and internationally.

Theofilos Tzanidis is a Senior Lecturer in Digital & 3DWeb Communications at University of the West of Scotland (UWS), where he develops and implements innovative strategies for engaging with current, future, and prospective stakeholders and partners. With over 20 years of experience in digital communications, he also leads the cross-faculty digital development team, designing and delivering cutting-edge digital platforms for teaching and learning in higher education. Theo is passionate about exploring and applying emerging technologies in the digital business transformation sector, such as reality technologies, AI for business, metaverse, Web3, and 3DWeb. He is currently involved in several digital transformation projects, aiming to cultivate new business competencies and opportunities in these domains. He is also a contributor to the World Economic Forum Agenda on metaverse, he is working closely with Meta, Google, Microsoft and Accenture as part of his project development and delivery of digital transformation themes, and a senior virtual/mixed reality and metaverse specialist at Eharo Ltd, an alternative investment management company specialised in Web3, AI, and related technologies.

Preface

The world is changing and bringing new fresh and innovative ideas. They are not just profitable, they are sociable, scalable and replicable along with being digital technological oriented. We are talking about the digital social entrepreneurship that embraces the digital technologies such as AI, metaverse, augmented reality, virtual realities, among others in the business model. These technologies are not just a tool to be used in the business but it is a crucial asset of the enterprise. Digital social entrepreneurship aims to generate social and environmental value not just for the local community but excessively for the rest of the world. A business born to be global and scalable. Digital social entrepreneurship is a peculiar business founded to help disadvantaged people such as not employed and not educated people, immigrants, people with physical disabilities, prisoners among others.

Today, all businesses need to be established considering social aims but digital social entrepreneurship completely relies on social goals, co-creation and embracement of digital technologies. It is relevant to generate social and sustainable value for the global community. A digital social enterprise scouts a social problem and then offers a social, innovative and digital solution made along with the collaboration of the external stakeholders involving citizens as well. À la Lumpkin and Bacq (2019), enterprises create communal and economic wealth creation but in this case, digital social enterprises also co-participate in the creation of social wealth that is associated with other external stakeholders such as universities, corporations, government agencies, among others. These stakeholders become relevant actors of the big project of digital social enterprises. They establish horizontal and collaborative networks to attract global talents and resources.

Digital social enterprises are assuming a key role in the entrepreneurial society. They improve quality of life for those disadvantaged people, offering new jobs, training, and competences. Overall, they offer a "new life" and a "new hope". They make structural and systemic changes, influencing policymakers and building new inclusive ecosystems, technology oriented. They make a social impact, generating a global engagement.

Acknowledgements

This study was funded by the European Union - NextGenerationEU, in the framework of the GRINS – Growing Resilient, INclusive and Sustainable project (GRINS PE00000018 – CUP E63C22002140007). The views and opinions expressed are solely those of the authors and do not necessarily reflect those of the European Union, nor can the European Union be held responsible for them.

Introduction

The book offers a deep overview of the topic "digital social entrepreneurship (DSE)". The authors examine the use of new technologies such as artificial intelligence, metaverse, and augmented reality to understand the evolution of social entrepreneurialism, considering three layers: micro, meso, and macro. The micro layer analyses digital social entrepreneurs' attitude in generating new digital social innovation for disadvantaged people such as not employed and not educated people; the meso layer explores the combination of digital and social initiatives in an entrepreneurial journey to improve inclusiveness and sustainability; and the macro layer investigates the impact of exogenous events on DSE to scaling such ventures, also offering an overview of disadvantaged entrepreneurs. The book is enriched by academic and professional insights on real cases of Digital Social Entrepreneurship.

Offering new insights, research, and practical guidance, this book will appeal in particular to scholars and post graduate students of entrepreneurship and small business management, organisational studies, technology, and innovation management.

The concept of Digital Social Entrepreneurship is outlined in five chapters. Each of them examines disadvantaged group of people considering entrepreneurs and\or citizens. They are structured as follows:

Chapter 1 explores the meaning of DSE including its different definitions and history. It offers a wide overview on such concepts, presenting when DSE was born and how it evolved. The chapter is enriched by the journey of a Digital Social Enterprise. This is a Story of Empowerment and Change, the vibrant heart of Bamako in Mali and then Ouagadougou, capital of Burkina Faso by Roberta d'Amore.

Chapter 2 looks inside the generation of digital social innovations offering a micro entrepreneurial perspective. It digs into the discussion of how to create social digital innovations in order to offer new scalable and replicable social solutions. The word "people" will be considered a central focus

DOI: 10.4324/9781003583448-1

in the process of making social innovations. A special case study Foreword is presented to describe a digital social innovation for deaf people.

Chapter 3 argues the embracement of Artificial Intelligences, Metaverse, and augmented reality in the DSE phenomenon. The use of such technologies explores a meso level, offering a deep overview of a combination of digital and social activities to offer rapid and more efficient solutions to the fast environmental changes. This chapter digs into the use of such technologies to support disadvantaged people.

Chapter 4[1] debates Digital Social Entrepreneurship and PPP implications from an SDG standpoint. First, it explores the historical and political context of the SDGs, tracing the evolution from the Bretton Woods era to contemporary challenges. Second, it analyses the regulatory and operational shortcomings of traditional PPPs. Third, it introduces social enterprises and details the transformative potential of DSEs as digital-native organisations. Fourth, it presents illustrative case studies from the People and Planet First database, highlighting practical applications of the DSE–PPP nexus. Finally, the chapter conceptualises this nexus as a new model of hybrid, digitally enabled governance for sustainable development, offering insights for academics, policymakers, and practitioners. By integrating geopolitical analysis, institutional critique, and real-world examples, the chapter provides a comprehensive framework for understanding and advancing SDG implementation through innovative, cross-sector partnerships.

Chapter 5 debates Digital Social Entrepreneurship and technological implications of scaling such ventures. This chapter explores the ever-evolving field of DSE, placing emphasis on the wider technological implications of efforts to scale up this type of venture. In doing so it suggests potential approaches to foster and develop an inclusive space that serves the needs of disadvantaged entrepreneurs. Three primary scaling strategies are examined here: scaling out, scaling up, and scaling deep and the ways in which each of these in turn is uniquely affected by digital technologies are examined here. Deliberate focus has been placed upon the specific barriers that may be encountered by disadvantaged entrepreneurs specifically in relation to accessing relevant digital technologies and a range of potential strategies that could be implemented to help build and create a more inclusive DSE ecosystem are identified. The conclusion offers a number of recommendations aimed at practitioners, policymakers, and researchers to help develop and foster a more inclusive DSE landscape that has the potential to more effectively address some of these social challenges while also attempting to ensure equitable participation across demographic groups and stakeholders is nurtured.

It ends offering valuable insights of a global business consultant Darin Bifani who talks about Scaling Digital Social Enterprises fully embracing inclusiveness and equality for underrepresented groups or in underrepresented regions, breaking language, digital, and social barriers.

Note

1 For the Chapter 4, the authors declare that they have used:

ChatGPT version 3.5, OpenAI: openai.com/chat. Helping with creation of text structure.

DeepL Translate, Deepl SE: deepl.com/translator. Translation of text passages.

NotebookLM, Google: notebooklm.google.com. Literature research, creation of summaries.

1 Digital Social Entrepreneurship

Origins and Evolutions

Veronica Scuotto

Digital Social Entrepreneurship, the State of the Art

When talking about new ventures and social missions it is commonly referring to social enterprises. The modern age along with the acceleration of the digital transformation has induced the development of new social enterprises that employ digital technologies such as artificial intelligence, machine learning, virtual reality, and so on. These enterprises are known as digital social enterprises. As for the social enterprises, the digital social enterprises are driven by a social mission but differently they are empowered by the use of new technologies (Short et al., 2009). Digital social enterprises are considered technology oriented (Ghatak et al., 2023) that interact with multiple agents and embrace technology in their business model (Yáñez-Valdés et al., 2023). The engagement and involvement of different actors form a N-helix that shape the type of collaborations and the networking approach (Ibáñez et al., 2022). It has also been defined as a linkage between private and public collaborations (Battisti, 2019). Digital social enterprises embrace multi -faceted entrepreneurial factors including institutional, knowledge, and business (Antonizzi & Smuts, 2020). These three factors express the capacity of the digital social entrepreneurship to exploit new opportunities and develop innovations (business entrepreneurship) (Muthukrishnan & Bhattacharyya, 2025); the ability to generate new knowledge (knowledge entrepreneurship) (Audretsch et al., 2020); the expertise of an entrepreneur to employ existing resources to establish new businesses and\or enhance existing ones (Hull et al., 2007; Ko & Liu, 2021). Yet, a digital social enterprise needs always to meet environmental, social, and governance (ESG) criteria. These criteria are relevant to assess the level of sustainability of the company, in terms of being responsible for the environment, generate a social impact that would influence governance practice. According to Zhiyang et al. (2020), digital social entrepreneurship is made of digital social entrepreneurs, digital social citizens, digital social entrepreneurship platforms and digital social regulation. These four elements recognise the value of this company to involve local community

DOI: 10.4324/9781003583448-2

(e.g. citizens) even though using the virtual environment (e.g. digital platforms) and being instructed by digital regulations. Overall, digital social entrepreneurship keeps its social nature and remains anchored to the social entrepreneurship structure (Yáñez-Valdés et al., 2023). It does not merely represent a modern variant of traditional social entrepreneurship, but a genuine evolution capable of generating scalable, inclusive, and sustainable impact through the strategic use of digital technologies. Digital social entrepreneurship intentionally adopts technologies as a key element of their business model.

The digital social enterprises are spread out throughout the whole world. For instance, in Italy, there is social business Italy that comes from Prof. Muhammad Yunus, who won the Nobel Peace prize in 2006. It offers a platform to put together all actors interested in improving the community's life. In this case, the main scope is to deal with hunger and poverty. Another digital social enterprise is "con i bambini" established in Rome and the scope is to deal with children's educational poverty. Rifo Lab is a digital social retailer and social fashion producer that employs the logic of the circular economy to preserve the environment and help local suppliers.

Digital social entrepreneurship emerges in a global context impacted by multiple crises such as climate change, socio-economic inequalities, migration, social polarisation, and educational and health challenges. These social problems are considered opportunities for social entrepreneurs in order to offer systemic responses. In this frame, the evolution and revolution of digital technologies has stimulated the shift of a traditional social enterprise into a digital one. Digital social entrepreneurship proposes itself as a concrete tool for activating hybrid solutions, founded on the capacity to innovate and include, exploiting the transformative potential of technology in a social key. Digital social entrepreneurship does not limit itself to digitalising existing processes, but radically rethinks the modalities of relationship with beneficiaries, service delivery, impact management, and value generation. It is an emerging model that deserves to be studied with attention, both for its capacity to respond to present needs and for its transformative potential in the long term.

From Social Entrepreneurship to a Digital Social Entrepreneurship

What distinguishes the entrepreneur from the ordinary economic operator is his attitude to risk and transformative leadership. He operates in conditions of uncertainty, where results are not predictable and the environment is not static. Schumpeter places particular emphasis on the importance of entrepreneurial personality: innovation does not occur due to technical necessity or automatic market dynamics, but thanks to the action of individuals capable of "making the leap", of breaking continuity. This vision has had a lasting impact on economic and entrepreneurial theory, laying the foundations for the modern understanding of entrepreneurship as a propulsive force of economic evolution. However, it is important to observe that, in Schumpeter's original formulation, innovation is conceived primarily in economic-productive terms and within a market logic oriented towards profit. Social purpose is not explicitly contemplated, nor is the way in which innovations impact on inclusion, equity, or sustainability problematised. The Schumpeterian entrepreneur operates within the boundaries of capitalism, with a focus centred on profit generation and competitive advantage. His action is transformative but not necessarily emancipatory: social impact is a possible consequence, not an objective. It is precisely on this point that contemporary reflection on social enterprise and the need for theoretical evolution is grafted. From the 1990s onwards, literature on social entrepreneurship has sought to broaden the Schumpeterian vision, integrating the concept of social mission with that of innovation. Authors such as Dees (1998) define the social entrepreneur as an individual who "pursues opportunities to create social value" rather than economic. In this perspective, risk, vision, and the capacity for transformation are preserved, but oriented towards objectives such as inclusion, social justice, and overcoming inequalities. Social innovation is thus configured as a form of "creative destruction for public purposes". This tension between systemic change and operational sustainability has led to the birth of hybrid models, which combine market practices with impact purposes. Social enterprise is positioned precisely in this intermediate space, adopting entrepreneurial techniques (such as revenue generation, strategic management, result orientation), but with the objective of producing relational, community, educational, or environmental goods, rather than exclusively economic ones (Defourny & Nyssens, 2008, 2010). Such enterprises aimed at environmental conservation along with social and economic inclusion. The key value proposition relies on ensuring that all individuals have the possibility of being fully and actively involved in our society. In turn, equitable access to resources, educational and employment opportunities, as well as health and social services for the entire population is also guaranteed. Such inclusion is relevant to face up poverty, income disparities, and unequal opportunities, as also addressed by the sustainable development goals. This has shaped the form of social entrepreneurship and then digital social entrepreneurship. As stated by Perrini and Vurro (2006), social entrepreneurship is

> a dynamic process created and managed by an individual or team (the innovative social entrepreneur), which strives to exploit social innovation with an entrepreneurial mindset and a strong need for achievement, in order to create new social value in the market and community at large.

This definition highlights some key elements of a social entrepreneur; first of all, the devotion to social mission that generates new innovations and, consequently, social value for the market and for the community. The authors also remark on the feature of being an innovative social entrepreneur and nurturing the entrepreneurial mindset. Mair and Martí (2006) declare that a social enterprise is recognised to be a process to create value by putting resources together in different ways. These resources are useful to explore and exploit external chances to address social needs and encourage social shift. This enterprise provides new products and\or service and also can establish new organisations. As Casson (2003) affirmed, an entrepreneur is able to coordinate scarce resources and generate value. The combination of exploring and exploiting, respectively implies the creation and evaluation of new potential advantages, using time and resources to identify alternatives and analyse market conditions, and induces the opportunity to take advantage of existing innovations so as to maximise benefits and costs. A social enterprise is considered a form of company focused on social impact and innovative methods to achieve its social mission. It is

> A set of innovative and effective activities that focus strategically on resolving social market failures and creating new opportunities to add social value systematically using a range of resources and organization formats to maximize social impact and bring about change.
>
> (Nicholls, 2010)

A social entrepreneur is a creative thinker who deals with social challenges so as to improve quality of life for a community. Hence, a social enterprise is social impact oriented with a high commitment towards the community's life. Martin and Osberg (2007) advance what could be considered as the most comprehensive definition of social entrepreneurship, in fact their work aims to definitively clarify who a social entrepreneur is and what actions they should implement to achieve the predetermined social objectives:

> We define Social Entrepreneurship as having the following three components: (1) identifying a stable but inherently unjust equilibrium that causes the exclusion, marginalization, or suffering of a segment of humanity that lacks the financial means or political clout to achieve any transformative benefit on its own; (2) identifying an opportunity in this unjust equilibrium, developing a social value proposition, and bringing to bear inspiration, creativity, direct action, courage, and fortitude, thereby challenging the stable state's hegemony; and (3) forging a new, stable equilibrium that releases trapped potential or alleviates the suffering of the targeted group, and through imitation and creation of a stable ecosystem around the new equilibrium ensuring a better future for the targeted group and even society at large.

The authors emphasise the need of establishing inclusivity in a context characterised by scarce resources and unequal distribution of them. The disequilibrium encourages the social entrepreneur to challenge the situation and triggers social change in order to achieve a state of equilibrium for the whole society.

However, modern society is driven by the continuous evolution and revolution of digital technologies. Such increasing digitalisation of society has led to a profound reconfiguration of entrepreneurial business models. In this scenario, digital social entrepreneurship emerges as a form of entrepreneurship that integrates the social intentionality typical of social enterprise with the strategic and structural use of digital technologies. This entrepreneurial model does not limit itself to modernising existing tools, but reformulates the processes of social value creation, proposing solutions that are more open, scalable, collaborative, and oriented towards inclusion. This form of a business embraces technologies as crucial assets for getting social and environmental value not just for the local community but for reaching extensively all. The digital social enterprise's business model seeks to be scalable and replicable. It is characterised by a social mission that aims to generate a positive impact for the community. It is driven by an entrepreneurial logic that is based on the capacity to sustain itself over time and generate innovation. It is digital technologies as structural levers for rethinking models of service, relationship, and impact. In this sense, digital technologies are integrated within a company and constitute the structural basis of the business model: from collaborative platforms to big data, from AI to blockchain, digital tools redesign the way of analysing needs, designing solutions, delivering services, and monitoring impact. Alongside, a digital social enterprise relies on a networking approach with beneficiaries, partners, and other stakeholders (e.g. public and private), surrounded by the objective of creating a social impact. In nutshell, digital social enterprises are born to respond to collective needs, reduce inequalities, and generate shared value, through digital solutions designed not for profit, but for widespread wellbeing. They combine economic sustainability and civic purposes, adopting flexible and scalable entrepreneurial business models, such as: Social freemium, Civic crowdfunding, Donation-based crowdfunding platform, Impact-as-a-Service, Peer-to-peer marketplaces and Advocacy platforms (see Table 1.1).

In this vein, knowledge and resources are shared, and value grows through generative interdependence, not competition. In turn, it stimulates the phenomenon of empowerment and community protagonism, seeking to stimulate people to be agents of change: disseminating skills, stimulating participation, favouring inclusion. Technology thus becomes an enabling infrastructure for active citizenship. This would provoke a systemic impact leading to structural transformations. If the advancement of digital technologies augments inequalities, a digital social enterprise offers

Table 1.1 Digital Social Entrepreneurial Business Models

Digital Social Entrepreneurial Business Model	*Description*	*References*
Social freemium	The Social Freemium business model leverages social programmes to convert free consumers to premium subscribers.	Belo and Li (2022)
Civic crowdfunding	"The most prominent themes in civic crowdfunding discourse are notions of participation, social equality and redistribution, and the role of government"	Davies (2015, p. 343)
Donation-based crowdfunding platform	"The term donation-based crowdfunding refers to a civic appeal that is instigated via the medium of web-assisted information systems wherein donations are made over a fixed, predetermined period of time"	Bhatt et al. (2025, p. 81)
Peer-to-peer marketplaces	The main goal is to help fragmented suppliers and buyers in the market. It aims to preserve local suppliers against corporations. It relies on sharing economy and community marketplace	Einav et al. (2016), Celata et al. (2017), Kyprianou (2018)
Social Sharing platforms	"Sharing platforms are said to facilitate positive impacts such as enhancing social cohesion, increasing trust in communities, empowering individuals, and increasing social ties among strangers".	Curtis et al. (2020, p. 4)
Advocacy platform	It is a digital platform that allows people and\or companies to recommend a cause, social idea, and so on in order to influence policymakers.	Hall et al. (2020)

an alternative model to reduce such inequalities and create innovations that can ameliorate living standards.

It is noticed that innovation is no longer centred on individual competition, but on distributed co-creation. Digital platforms enable collaboration processes between public, private, and civic actors; they favour the scalability of solutions and knowledge sharing; and they build enabling ecosystems in which the entrepreneur is not only a solitary agent, but part of a broader network. This post-Schumpeterian approach recovers the idea of "new combinations", but declines them in relational and participatory terms.

Digital Social Entrepreneurship versus Other Forms of Sustainable Entrepreneurship

Digital Social Entrepreneurship is not simply limited to the use of digital technologies but it has profoundly been redefining the way of thinking, acting, and producing social impact. Technology is no longer just a means to support social intervention, but becomes a central component of innovation itself: it enables new forms of collaboration, favours the scalability of solutions, allows real-time impact monitoring, and opens spaces for co-design with heterogeneous communities and stakeholders.

Similarly to a traditional social enterprise, a digital social enterprise is featured by an hybrid model that integrates economic efficiency with social and community purposes. It addresses complex challenges that neither the public sector nor the market have managed to fully resolve. Wu et al. (2020) define a social enterprise as an hybrid business that serves "as a vehicle for social engagement" with the scope to generate social value by exploiting resources, business, and innovation. This definition can be generally used to describe a digital social enterprise that also uses digital technologies.

In addition, this form of a business can be distinguished with benefit society, ecopreneurship and B-corporations. According to Lenzi (2016), the benefit society model was introduced in the Italian entrepreneurial landscape to solve socio-environmental issues. In turn, this form of a business aims to stimulate the interests in preserving local territory and supporting the local community. It combines economic growth, social well-being, and environmental protection. This form of environmental preservation is linked to the figure of the ecopreneurship that

> Is a combination of two words, 'ecological' ('eco') and 'entrepreneurship'. Ecopreneurship can thus be roughly defined as 'entrepreneurship through an environmental lens'. Ecopreneurship is characterised by some fundamental aspects of entrepreneurial activities that are oriented less towards management systems or technical procedures and focused more on the personal initiative and skills of the entrepreneurial person or team to realise market success with environmental innovations.
>
> (Schaltegger, 2002, p. 39)

In this context, even the corporations are offering innovative solutions to improve the community's life. This is known as B-Corp certification. Its main objective is to promote a more inclusive and sustainable economy through the development and dissemination of standards of social and environmental responsibility for businesses, a goal pursued through the creation of the B-Corp certification. The B-Corp certification guarantees the company's commitment to pursuing collective well-being objectives that go beyond the mere purpose of individual profit, integrating social and environmental benefits into its business. It is "a badge signals to others that the company adheres to these standards and may enhance reputations and increase business from socially conscious consumers" (Villela et al., 2021, p. 344) (Table 1.2).

Table 1.2 Forms of Sustainable Entrepreneurship. Created by the Author

Forms of Sustainable Entrepreneurship	*Definition*	*References*
Digital social entrepreneurship	Digital social enterprises are considered technology oriented, that interact with multiple agents and embrace technology in their business model. Their main mission is pursuing social goals.	Yáñez-Valdés et al. (2023)
Social entrepreneurship	Social entrepreneurship is "a dynamic process created and managed by an individual or team (the innovative social entrepreneur), which strives to exploit social innovation with an entrepreneurial mindset and a strong need for achievement, in order to create new social value in the market and community at large".	Perrini & Vurro (2006)
Benefit society	The benefit society model was introduced in the Italian entrepreneurial landscape to solve socio-environmental issues.	Lenzi (2016)
Ecopreneurship	This is a combination of two words, 'ecological' ('eco') and 'entrepreneurship'. Ecopreneurship can thus be roughly defined as 'entrepreneurship through an environmental lens'. Ecopreneurship is characterised by some fundamental aspects of entrepreneurial activities that are oriented less towards management systems or technical procedures and focused more on the personal initiative and skills of the entrepreneurial person or team to realise market success with environmental innovations".	Schaltegger (2002)
B-Corporations	"Certification as a badge signals to others that the company adheres to these standards and may enhance reputations and increase business from socially conscious consumers".	Villela et al. (2021)

Digital Social Entrepreneurship (DSE) represents a qualitative evolution of social entrepreneurship, which does not limit itself to integrating digital technologies into existing models, but gives shape to new modalities of collective action and social impact organisation. For the authors, DSE is not simply a technological update of traditional social enterprise, but rather an emerging phenomenon that is founded on different logics: collaboration instead of centralisation, flexibility instead of structural rigidity, co-creation instead of top-down planning. In this model, impact is no longer produced by a single actor, but emerges from collaborative networks, from the circulation of knowledge, and from the capacity to exploit distributed resources within an ecosystem. A central element of Chalmers and Shaw's vision relies on the role of the actors which are constantly modified. Hence, the digital social enterprise is enforced by the involvement of a dynamic process supported by technologies that facilitate transparency, interaction, and adaptability. Digital social entrepreneurship should not just be considered an updated version of traditional social entrepreneurship because it has its own business model that drives the achievement and measurement of the social impact (Zhiyang et al., 2020). This form of a business allows a better inclusive approach, offering transparent communications and bottom -up approach. It tries to overcome the increasing digital gap that traditional companies cannot face alone. Traditional social enterprises tend to treat beneficiaries as recipients of their actions. Even if participatory practices exist, the relationship often remains asymmetric: those who design and those who receive do not coincide. On the contrary, DSE tends to overcome this logic, proposing models of co-creation, crowdsourcing, peer-to-peer learning, and other forms of active community involvement. Knowledge becomes distributed, and social impact is generated together with users, not only for them. Social impact is a central objective for both forms of entrepreneurship, but the modalities with which it is generated and measured change radically. Traditional enterprises often struggle to collect systematic data, relying on qualitative indicators or ex-post evaluations. Digital enterprises collect big data in real time, track user engagement, personalise interactions, and measure programme effectiveness through dashboards and advanced monitoring systems. Furthermore, digital social enterprises are generally oriented towards scalability, precisely because digital allows replicating models and distributing them on a large scale with minimal marginal costs. An educational platform can be translated, adapted, and disseminated globally in rapid times, whilst a traditional social enterprise often requires physical presence and local human resources. This difference also translates into a different logic of sustainability.

In summary, Digital Social Entrepreneurship does not replace, but redefines social entrepreneurship, expanding its possibilities through new tools, models, and relationships. If traditional social enterprise has represented the human and local response to collective needs, DSE aspires to build inclusive and scalable digital ecosystems, in which technology becomes infrastructure for impact. The two visions are not necessarily in conflict, but can be complementary: one anchored to proximity and relationship, the other projected towards innovation and network.

Conclusions

The concept of entrepreneurship has been studied for ages. There is a wave of theories from Marshall in the 19th century to Schumpeter passing by Cantillon, Drucker, Kirzner, Casson, and so on. Marshall considers an entrepreneur as who uses resources in the best way; Kirzner talks about creative alertness referring to the capacity of an entrepreneur to exploit new opportunities, Drucker states that an entrepreneur foresees new market trends. Later to them, Schumpeter introduced the term "creative destruction" in the way that entrepreneurs generate innovation (Block et al., 2017; Malerba & McKelvey, 2020). All of them declare that an entrepreneur pursues profit. However, with the acceleration of the digital transformation and globalisation that have augmented social disparities and problems, the need to deal with these challenges has become more pervasive. This has induced the birth of social enterprises first, and then digital social enterprises (Prodanov, 2018; Ghatak et al., 2023). Schumpeter's vision can be reconsidered in this scenario. The digital social entrepreneur embodies the Schumpeterian attitude to disrupt and change, translating new combinations of resources into organisational models, platforms, and innovative services. Although this form of entrepreneurship has a hybrid model that prioritises the achievement of a social impact, it is also oriented to profit maximisation. The process of innovation is not only economic efficiency, but is the capacity to produce inclusive and sustainable systemic transformations. As the world economic forum (2025) highlights, social entrepreneurship "lies in its versatility". It brings different agents together to solve social problems. The digital divide is still a big issue that generates inequalities and so there is a matter if digital social innovations can increase such disparities. Likely, real cases of companies demonstrate that digital social entrepreneurs are dealing with this gap, offering new digital training for not employed, educated and training (NEET) people. For instance, the Politecnico of Milan has launched the project PROXIMO to help young people who are in the condition to become NEET. In the Netherlands, SOCIALNEET provides the integration of young people categorised as NEET in the labour market. Again, SOSUK project is aimed at "European youngsters "as NEET, offering them social and green entrepreneurship skills.

Their strength relies on the networking approach and the involvement of the ecosystem (Box 1.1). A lonely Individual initiative is not enough: shared infrastructures, access to public data, tax incentives, acceleration programmes, and public policies oriented towards impact are needed. In this realm, entrepreneurs, activists, policymakers, and ecosystem actors need to guarantee that technology is a means to be more efficient and innovative. Furthermore, the digital environment favours accessible and modular training, which can contribute to the empowerment of the most vulnerable groups. Digital social entrepreneurship is a promising tool to address these complexities in an innovative and sustainable manner by the employment of digital technologies.

Box 1.1 Case Study

My Journey into Digital Social Enterprise: A Story of Empowerment and Change

Roberta d'Amore

Crafting stories and change | Social Entrepreneur | Working for Girls' Education and Women's Rights

Founder @ Dambé

It is strange how life, in the end, managed to get me where, deep in my heart, I always knew it would be. I am not necessarily talking about a physical place, but my place in the world. My name is Roberta d'Amore, and I'd like to share my journey, a journey that took me from Italy to the vibrant heart of Bamako in Mali and then Ouagadougou, capital of Burkina Faso. In September 2021, I joined my husband Francesco in Mali, a long-cherished dream that finally came true when the stars aligned just right.

Before this adventure, I spent years in the communications field, starting at 23 in a press office in Rome, then moving to a local news station, which I absolutely loved. Life took me to California and then to Amsterdam, where I worked for a fashion brand. Those years were intense and unforgettable, but deep down, I felt a strong urge for change.

Once I arrived in Mali, I did not speak French. But I quickly adapted to my new surroundings trying to fit into the context through a language everyone loves: food! I launched a small catering business focused on Italian home cooking. When I started, I didn't think it would go so well. Social media has been crucial. I started posting pictures of recipes and weekly menus on Instagram, slowly the word spread. The boom came when the news of a Neapolitan woman cooking at home in Bamako appeared on a popular whatsapp group! This small business revived my passion for cooking and allowed me to embrace a slower rhythm of life while working with my hands. It also provided job opportunities for local young men who delivered our meals on scooters.

With the earnings from my catering business, I've started buying fabrics. In Mali, there's a beautiful tradition of hand-dyed and woven fabrics, like bogolan and indigo. Plus, there are the colourful and widely used wax-printed cottons!

I met a talented seamstress, Aminata, and we've begun collaborating to start a small tailoring workshop. Fashion has always been a passion of mine, but **my true desire was to create something meaningful for women**. The most rewarding part of this journey has been seeing Aminata use her earnings to purchase two sewing machines and open her own lab, where she now works and teaches to other girls the craft (Figure 1.1).

Figure 1.1 Aminata. Photograph by the Author.

In the lab I set up at home has started to work Clarisse, a young girl who worked with us twice a week. She's a talented seamstress, but her heart is set on becoming a nurse one day. Thanks to her earnings, she supports her family and has even been able to buy materials for nursing school. Dambé, our tailoring workshop, is more than just a business; it's a space where women can forge their own futures through their work.

Initially, my vision was to create handmade clothing and accessories that tell stories of freedom and empowerment. Each piece we produce carries the narrative of women who have transformed their lives through hard work and determination.

However, my heart often wandered to the children of Bamako. The educational crisis in Mali is alarming, with over 1,700 schools closed and more than two million children out of school, particularly affecting girls who face even greater challenges. I knew I had to take action.

I decided to raise funds to cover school fees for vulnerable children and girls, believing that education is the key to independence. I started by identifying ten children in need of support for their school fees, uniforms, and supplies. I made it a point to ensure they were enrolled and thriving in school. So far, I've raised funds for 20 children and supported Clarisse and Marie in nursing school (Figure 1.2).

Figure 1.2 Capturing a moment of lecturing. Photograph by the Author.

For the upcoming school year, we're also helping six girls from the Jiriladon dancing company, who have faced significant difficulties. This company was founded by Fatoumata Bagayoko, who is a dancer and choreographer from Bamako. Fatoumata is not just a talented artist; she's also a brave woman deeply involved in her community. She created Jiriladon as a way to empower girls and children in her neighbourhood. The name "Jiriladon" actually means a new tree that grows using the roots of a big tree, symbolising growth in the modern world. Through dance, she's standing up against the issues and taboos she's faced herself. The girls who join her company have often experienced various forms of abuse, including female genital mutilation, early marriages, and physical and psychological violence. They're girls who are denied the right to education and are made to believe that their only role is to cook and reproduce.

Fatoumata told me that her family has belonged to the *forgerons* (metalworkers) for generations. According to oral tradition, Malian society is divided into 30 families based on belonging to a common ancestor: *les hommes libres, les griots, les marabouts, les artisans, les forgerons* (free men, storytellers, marabouts, artisans, metalworkers) and many others. It is a system common to many West African countries, such as Burkina Faso, Senegal or Guinea, similar to caste system and corresponds to a social stratification that still exists today and dates back to the time when Mali was an empire.

In the culture of the forgerons, the oldest man in the family decides whether women should undergo excision. There are various reasons for this: firstly, there is a desire to subjugate or reduce female sexuality. Then there are sociological reasons related to community cohesion, religious, sanitary, hygienic and aesthetic reasons.

I discussed the topic of female genital mutilation with Caroline Muller, project coordinator for UNFPA (United Nations Fund for Population Activities): female mutilation is a widespread and complex phenomenon involving the partial or total removal of the female external genitalia. In Mali, the percentage of women who undergo this practice is 89%, in an age range of 15–49 years and 74% of girls in an age range of 0–14 years. In some areas of Mali, according to surveys of the population's perceptions and beliefs, the female organ is referred to as the devil organ. Mutilation is therefore intended to control women's sexuality, which is not to be free. In addition to this phenomenon, there is the reality of early marriages; girls forced to marry before the age of 15 and in 53% of cases even before the age of eight. In Mali, genital mutilation and child marriage are not criminalised. A draft law criminalising these practices along with other forms of gender-based violence, was proposed in 2017, but was not passed. However, UNFPA, UNICEF and various national and international actors are continuing a strong advocacy campaign to ban all forms of gender-based violence in Mali but to date, unfortunately, there are still no laws to hinder their practice. Worldwide, the number of women living with this wound is several million. Children, girls, women who suffer serious and irreversible physical and psychological damage.

Fatoumata has chosen dance as a tool to react and to raise awareness in her community, her family, the people around her, and public opinion. Dance as a tool to express herself, to overcome a trauma. She chose to fight for herself and to ensure a better future for the girls in her neighbourhood. She clashed with her family and challenged part of her community that did not believe in the change she is stubbornly pursuing. Through training and practising traditional dances, the girls who were lucky enough to meet her found a constructive way out of their pain. A way to express themselves, believe in themselves and above all convince themselves that they deserve a better life (Figure 1.3).

I was inspired by what Fatoumata had created, and I realised that believing in these girls and investing in their education was the best way for them to ensure their future and help them to become independent. Five girls are enrolled in the beauty school, and one is in the technolab course. They are excited to learn a profession and study. This was the opportunity they had been waiting for. The hardest thing I realised is that these girls are invisible. They feel they are not seen. What they ask, or rather rightly demand, is to be able to study, to be able to create a future for themselves through their work. To be able to be independent, to be able to choose what is right for them to do with their own lives.

Choosing to support them means creating a movement of change that shows how economic and social empowerment can lead to a fairer, more supportive and inclusive future. Each success story fuels hope and inspires other women to believe in their own abilities, showing that true power comes from determination, solidarity and the will to change the rules of the game. Through their work, they are proving that economic independence can be a powerful tool for empowerment (Figure 1.4).

According to UN Women data, about 70% of women in Mali live in poverty and have limited access to education and health

Figure 1.3 Girl dancing from Jiriladon association. Photograph by the Author.

Figure 1.4 Women empowerment. Photograph by the Author.

services. Female participation in the labour market is still very low, and women often face cultural and social barriers that hinder their personal and professional development. That is why I believe that we must start with education, especially of girls, who unfortunately, just because they are born girls, are the most vulnerable category.

To ensure these children can continue their education, I've created a piggy bank for future fees and to assist with additional costs like school meals and transportation. Transparency is key; I share updates about the children's progress with everyone involved in this initiative.

Living in Mali has opened my eyes to the challenges many face, and I'm committed to creating positive change. I'm grateful for the impact we're making in the lives of children, girls, and their families. Dambé started as a way for me to give back for the blessings I've received, but it has blossomed into a community effort fuelled by love and the belief that we can change the world.

In just three years, we've achieved remarkable milestones:

- Twenty children (11 girls and 9 boys) are enrolled in school.
- Eight girls are enrolled in the training school.
- Two girls graduated.
- Four hundred children from the school in Konsogou-De, in a village in the Dogon countries, received a supply of exercise books and pens for the entire school year.

I know I am a droplet in the ocean, but in this context, I believe this project is an illustration of how women's work is an example of how economic empowerment can translate into wider social change (Figures 1.5 and 1.6).

Each woman who succeeds in becoming independent and sharing her skills with others contributes to a more equitable and inclusive environment, giving hope to many others to follow her example.

Their example reminds us that change starts from within, that every woman has the power to be the protagonist of her own life and to positively influence the community. It is a universal message that transcends borders and cultures: the power of women is an engine of progress, hope, and peace.

I believe it is the responsibility of each of us to take care of the world we live in, not just our own little piece. Children are the society of tomorrow: which country can be a country where men and women cannot read and write, where there are not enough doctors to care for the population, where there are not enough teachers and professors. A country in which children cannot dream, has no future.

Figure 1.5 A teacher with her students in a classroom in Bamako. Photograph by the Author.

In conclusion, I want to emphasise that the success of my project would not have been achievable without the incredible power of social media. These platforms have revolutionised the way we share stories, create communities and generate change. For me, social media has been the bridge that has connected my actions in Mali with a global audience, allowing me to raise awareness, gather support and inspire others to believe in the power of collective change. This sense of connection has made every step of this journey even more meaningful.

Through Instagram, WhatsApp, and other platforms, I have been able to tell the stories of the women and children we support, bringing to light realities that are often invisible and forgotten. The ability to share images, videos, and updates in real time has created a sense of closeness and participation that transcends geographical distances. This connection has fuelled a network of solidarity, allowing us to mobilise quickly and involve people from all over the world, all united by a desire to make a difference, creating a

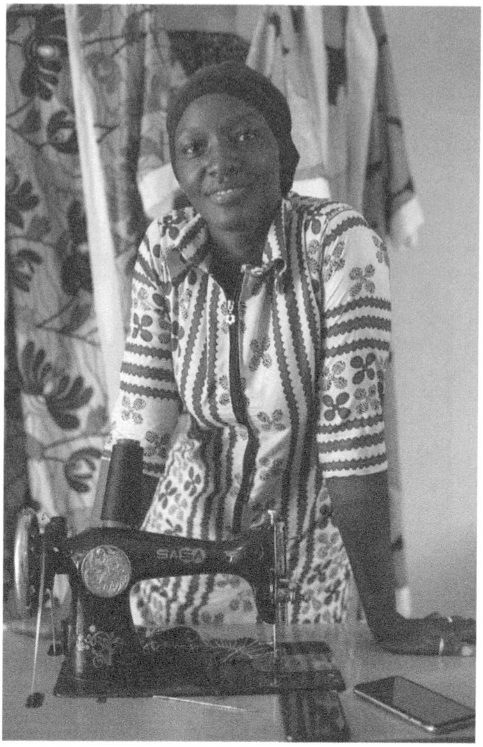

Figure 1.6 A seamstress at work in the atelier in Bamako, part of the Dambé project. Photograph by the Author.

dialogue that transcends geographical boundaries. This is a testament to the positive impact that social media can have on society. It has the potential to change lives by amplifying voices, spreading awareness, and inspiring action: social media has also given voice to those who would otherwise have remained silent: women, girls, and children who can now tell their stories, express their dreams and ask for help. This democratisation of communication has made possible an authentic and direct dialogue that strengthens the sense of community and shared responsibility.

In addition, newsletters and digital campaigns have allowed me to maintain transparency and constant engagement, sharing the progress and challenges of our journey. This approach has strengthened trust and motivated many people to actively support our initiatives, proving that change can start with a simple click and a sincerely shared message.

Ultimately, social media has become a key tool to amplify the voices of those fighting for a better future, creating a global movement of hope and action. I am deeply grateful to all those who shared this adventure with me, because together we proved that stories, when shared with passion and authenticity, can truly change the world, and that when we come together, we can truly make a difference (Figure 1.7).

Figure 1.7 Dambè community. Photograph by the Author.

References

Antonizzi, J., & Smuts, H. (2020). The characteristics of digital entrepreneurship and digital transformation: A systematic literature review. In *Responsible Design, Implementation and Use of Information and Communication Technology: 19th IFIP WG 6.11 Conference on e-Business, e-Services, and e-Society, I3E 2020, Skukuza, South Africa*, April 6–8, 2020, Proceedings, Part I 19 (pp. 239–251). Springer International Publishing.

Audretsch, D. B., Belitski, M., Caiazza, R., & Lehmann, E. E. (2020). Knowledge management and entrepreneurship. *International Entrepreneurship and Management Journal*, 16(2), 373–385.

Battisti, S. (2019). Digital social entrepreneurs as bridges in public–private partnerships. *Journal of Social Entrepreneurship*, 10(2), 135–158.

Belo, R., & Li, T. (2022). Social referral programs for freemium platforms. *Management Science*, 68(12), 8933–8962.

Bhatt, V., Pandey, S., Patel, R., Ghodake, S., Jariwala, H., & Thomas, S. (2025). Predicting online donation intention in donation-based crowdfunding apps: A multi-stage SEM-ANN-NCA model integrating anthropomorphism, satisfaction, trust, and privacy concerns. *Journal of Nonprofit & Public Sector Marketing*, 37(1), 80–104.

Block, J. H., Fisch, C. O., & Van Praag, M. (2017). The Schumpeterian entrepreneur: A review of the empirical evidence on the antecedents, behaviour and consequences of innovative entrepreneurship. *Industry and Innovation*, 24(1), 61–95.

Casson, M. (2003). The entrepreneur: An economic theory. In *The Entrepreneur*. Edward Elgar Publishing.

Celata, F., Hendrickson, C.Y., & Sanna, V.S. (2017). The sharing economy as community marketplace? Trust, reciprocity and belonging in peer-to-peer accommodation platforms. *Cambridge Journal of Regions, Economy and Society*, 10(2), 349–363.

Curtis, S. K., Singh, J., Mont, O., & Kessler, A. (2020). Systematic framework to assess social impacts of sharing platforms: Synthesising literature and stakeholder perspectives to arrive at a framework and practice-oriented tool. *PloS One*, 15(10), e0240373.

Davies, R. (2015). Three provocations for civic crowdfunding. *Information, Communication & Society*, *18*(3), 342–355.

Dees, J. G. (1998, October). The meaning of social entrepreneurship.

Defourny, J., & Nyssens, M. (2008). Social enterprise in Europe: Recent trends and developments. *Social Enterprise Journal*, 4(3), 202–228.

Defourny, J., & Nyssens, M. (2010). Conceptions of social enterprise and social entrepreneurship in Europe and the United States: Convergences and divergences. *Journal of Social Entrepreneurship*, 1(1), 32–53.

Einav, L., Farronato, C., & Levin, J. (2016). Peer-to-peer markets. *Annual Review of Economics*, 8(1), 615–635.

Ghatak, A., Chatterjee, S., & Bhowmick, B. (2023). Intention towards digital social entrepreneurship: An integrated model. *Journal of Social Entrepreneurship*, 14(2), 131–151.

Hall, N., Schmitz, H. P., & Dedmon, J. M. (2020). Transnational advocacy and NGOs in the digital era: New forms of networked power. *International Studies Quarterly*, 64(1), 159–167.

Hull, C. E. K., Hung, Y. T. C., Hair, N., Perotti, V., & DeMartino, R. (2007). Taking advantage of digital opportunities: A typology of digital entrepreneurship. *International Journal of Networking and Virtual Organisations*, 4(3), 290–303.

Ibáñez, M. J., Guerrero, M., Yáñez-Valdés, C., & Barros-Celume, S. (2022). Digital social entrepreneurship: The N-Helix response to stakeholders' COVID-19 needs. *The Journal of Technology Transfer*, 47(2), 556–579.

Ko, W. W., & Liu, G. (2021). The transformation from traditional nonprofit organizations to social enterprises: An institutional entrepreneurship perspective. *Journal of Business Ethics*, 171(1), 15–32.

Kyprianou, C. (2018). Creating value from the outside in or the inside out: How nascent intermediaries build peer-to-peer marketplaces. *Academy of Management Discoveries*, 4(3), 336–370.

Lenzi, D. (2016). Le società benefit. *Giurisprudenza Commerciale*, 6(1), 894–920.

Mair, J., & Martí, I. (2006). Social entrepreneurship research: A source of explanation, prediction, and delight. *Journal of World Business*, 41(1), 36–44.

Malerba, F., & McKelvey, M. (2020). Knowledge-intensive innovative entrepreneurship integrating Schumpeter, evolutionary economics, and innovation systems. *Small Business Economics*, 54(2), 503–522.

Martin, R. L., & Osberg, S. (2007). Social entrepreneurship: The case for definition. *Stanford Social Innovation Review*, 29–39.

Muthukrishnan, U., & Bhattacharyya, S. S. (2025). Charting the boundaries of digital social entrepreneurship and proposing an outlook. *Social Enterprise Journal*, ahead-of-print No. ahead-of-print. https://doi.org/10.1108/SEJ-11-2024-0174

Nicholls, A. (2010). The legitimacy of social entrepreneurship: Reflexive isomorphism in a pre–paradigmatic field. *Entrepreneurship Theory and Practice*, 34(4), 611–633.

Perrini, F., & Vurro, C. (2006). Social entrepreneurship: Innovation and social change across theory and practice. In *Social Entrepreneurship* (pp. 57–85). London: Palgrave Macmillan Springer Nature Link, UK.

Prodanov, H. (2018). Social entrepreneurship and digital technologies. *Economic Alternatives*, 1(1), 123–138.

Schaltegger, S. (2002). A framework for ecopreneurship: Leading bioneers and environmental managers to ecopreneurship. *Greener Management International*, (38), 45–58. https://www.jstor.org/stable/greemanainte.38.45?casa_token=7LIXLOV6Le4AAAAA%3AEhaPfmxNIUy8TQdHu--IEUt1NAoyE0ZONib_e0xVkR_wBnkLCGXhO2BoeNIJXF6uIWeCzgSP2rYJWHXf19uXuB1D5shrsvjT7wHKKr3w3RbayfQO&seq=1

Short, J. C., Moss, T. W., & Lumpkin, G. T. (2009). Research in social entrepreneurship: Past contributions and future opportunities. *Strategic Entrepreneurship Journal*, 3(2), 161–194.

Villela, M., Bulgacov, S., & Morgan, G. (2021). B Corp certification and its impact on organizations over time. *Journal of Business Ethics*, 170, 343–357.

World Economic Forum (2025). Social entrepreneurship and innovation has moved from the margins to the mainstream. Retrieved from https://www.weforum.org/stories/2025/01/social-innovation-has-moved-from-the-margins-to-the-mainstream/ on the 20th February 2025.

Wu, Y. J., Wu, T., & Arno Sharpe, J. (2020). Consensus on the definition of social entrepreneurship: A content analysis approach. *Management Decision*, 58(12), 2593–2619.

Yáñez-Valdés, C., Guerrero, M., Barros-Celume, S., & Ibáñez, M. J. (2023). Winds of change due to global lockdowns: Refreshing digital social entrepreneurship research paradigm. *Technological Forecasting and Social Change*, 190, 122454.

Zhiyang, L., Chenfang, Z., & Bin, L. (2020). Digital social entrepreneurship: Theoretical framework and research outlook. *Foreign Economics & Management*, 42(04), 3–18.

2 Generating Digital Social Innovations

Veronica Scuotto

From Social Innovation…

The concept of innovation has been largely studied (Kahn, 2018; Drucker, 2002). Schumpeter (1934) distinguishes innovation from incremental to radical. Before that, this concept is differentiated with the term invention because innovation refers to the commercialisation stage of an innovation.

An invention can stay as a discovery and never be transformed into an innovation but to let that invention be used and purchased by other people, it needs to become an innovation, that means a product and\or service that can be commercialised. It generates a demand and an offer.

Innovation is also further distinguished in incremental and radical innovation. Incremental innovation refers to the existing products that are improved (e.g. from Apple smartphone first version to the recent one); while radical innovation regards products that are completely new and disrupt the current market situation (e.g. internet, artificial intelligence, metaverse, etc.). Innovations were also associated with the involvement of different actors (e.g. open innovation by Chesbrough, Vanhaverbeke & West, 2014). Although it is noticed that Schumpeterian theories rely on maximising profit, Croitoru (2019) offers a different lens of Schumpeter's thoughts remarking the sustainable and community orientation. He affirms that the approach of new combinations or disrupting existing equilibriums can be adopted in social contexts as well. In the social context, entrepreneurial creativity relies on the sense of inclusiveness, community well-being and social cohesion. In turn, innovation is not just a way to generate profit but also the means to offer new benefits to communities.

Such a socially remarkable aspect of this innovation has stimulated new studies. The Stanford graduate business school has analysed the term innovation along with the concept of social. Innovation is considered as a process and it is based on individual creativity and it is influenced by social and economic factors and external contexts. While, the concept of social regards an outcome that is obtained by the realisation of a product or a service or a process that aims to meet social needs for a community

DOI: 10.4324/9781003583448-3

(for example, justice, equity, and environmental preservation). Ramani et al. (2017) declare that innovation needs to be studied not just considering its economic impact but also its social consequences.

In turn, innovation becomes social and it has spurred several studies on social innovation (van der Have & Rubalcaba, 2016; Philips et al., 2015). According to Bacq and Janssen (2011) social innovations are "innovative solutions to [the] social problems of his/her community that are not adequately met by the local system" (p. 382).

In this context, innovation assumes the form of social innovation since they are generated to solve social problems and get a balance between preserving the environment and inclusivity. For instance, if people look after the environment, the quality of life can be improved. This requests the involvement of different actors in generating new business ideas. Indeed, social innovation generates new ideas that address social problems and meet social needs through the creation of social networking (European Commission, 2013). It involves the whole society in the process of idea generation. Social innovation takes in account social conditions "social conditions in which it is produced both in terms of its purpose and its effects and methods". Social innovation needs a strong ecosystem to generate new ideas. It is promoted as a means for enhancing economic growth and employment, supporting innovative entrepreneurs and mobilising investors through public funds. The concept of social innovation was also studied by the Stanford Graduate School of Business in 2008, it was asserted that "A social innovation is a novel solution to a social problem that is more effective, efficient, sustainable, or just than current solutions. The value created accrues primarily to society rather than to private individuals". In this case, the effect of the new innovation is towards not just a single individual but for a society.

It requests an unconventional approach to solve social problems. It relies on the effectiveness in solving a social problem, efficiency in the use of resources, sustainability in environmental and organisational terms, and justice in the equitable distribution of benefits for the community.

The European commission affirms that social innovation is based on

> New solutions (products, services, models, process, etc.) that simultaneously meet a social need, more effectively than existing solutions and lead to new or improved capabilities and relationships and better use of assets or resources. In other words, social innovations are both good for society and enhance society's capacity to act.

Differently from the definition of innovation, social innovation is substantiated by a networking approach. The ecosystem actors assume a crucial role in the process of idea generation.

The role of the community is then fundamental, which is actively involved through social innovation, allowing the direct participation of local communities, organisations, and other actors in the process of developing and implementing such solutions. Inclusivity drives such innovations so as to guarantee a democratic access and benefits to all individuals, including disadvantaged or usually marginalised groups.

It makes possible the improvement of human living conditions by facilitating communication, promotes the improvement of conditions and safety in the workplace, as well as ensuring respect for the environment through new production processes to drastically reduce pollution, allowing savings of natural and energy resources. Hence, social innovation favours the creation of new economic models that integrate social and environmental objectives with the creation of economic value, in order to facilitate the transition towards a more sustainable economy. This has stimulated the interest between social innovation and entrepreneurship (Bacq & Eddleston, 2018; Bhatt et al., 2019; El-Haddadehn et al., 2014). Tracey and Stott (2017) state that social innovations generate and develop new solutions to face social issues, whose benefits go beyond the mere fact of generating profit. As said before, it has stimulated new studies that have highlighted the social innovation nature based on collective purpose (Phills et al., 2008), a response to government welfare state failure (Murray et al., 2010), and relational and transformative dimension (European Commission, 2013). Hence, if innovation seems to be profit-oriented, not considering the mutual and collective impact; the social innovation is founded on the principles of inclusion, justice, social cohesion, and democratisation. It fosters collective construction of transformative human capacities and democratises the innovation process, involving people from the bottom like citizens and clients. It also engages with local actors, embracing cultural diversity and relational capital. This becomes a participatory response to social problems with the participation of local actors such as institutions, citizens and organisations.

To Digital Social Innovation

Going more specifically, the discussion on the social innovation connected with the digital technologies induces new explorations to understand how to preserve our planet and human beings from environmental conservation to inclusivity. Environmental conservation is essential to ensure the survival of all forms of life on Earth, including humanity itself. The balance of biodiversity, air and water quality, and the protection of nature represent key elements in safeguarding the existence of all human beings on our planet. The relevance of preserving biodiversity can improve the stability of the ecosystem and offer a better environment for future generations. This requires a huge effort and cooperation among people. Inclusivity is crucial for both social and economic sides. It is a necessity to guarantee that all individuals have the possibility of being fully and actively involved in our society. Alongside that all people feel to be part of the same society even if they belong to a different social class or come from another country. This calls for social inclusion and so ensuring equitable access to resources, educational and employment opportunities, as well as health and social services for the entire population. The scope of social innovation is also to guarantee inclusivity to reduce cultural differences, poverty, and income disparities. As already widely promoted by the United Nations through the sustainable development goals (SDGs), all countries have to offer decent working conditions, sufficient income, and adequate social support is crucial for building an equitable society.

However, studies on the impact and\or role of technologies on social innovations are still limited (Charalabidis et al., 2014; Qureshi et al., 2021). Qureshi et al. (2021) affirm this lack of studies unveils the need to offer new research on this field including the role of entrepreneurs as well.

Digital social innovation refers to the adoption of new digital technologies to generate new ideas that can improve community's life and address social problems (Edwards-Schachter & Wallace, 2017). This innovation tends to improve "well-being and agency of socially disadvantaged groups or address social problems related to marginality, inequality and social exclusion" (Qureshi, Pan, & Zheng, 2021; Shalini et al., 2025). Even if digital social innovation can be confused with technological innovation, it prioritizes the social characteristics of an innovation such as sustainable solutions, solving social problems, and meeting social needs. It can be an innovation based on the blockchain or a platform but should bring new benefits for the community and help disadvantaged people. For instance, Torino city lab is a civic engagement platform for citizens in order to get them involved in the decision making process of the city. They can suggest new ideas, address and present social problems. This platform works thanks to the cooperation with the whole ecosystem composed of banks, investors, entrepreneurs, government and non-government organizations, foundations and so on. Similarly, in Belgium there is CitizenLab to co-create a city with citizens' involvement. In the UK, open voice factory is a digital social innovation to improve communication with disadvantaged people. This platform "makes communication aids more accessible by producing a free and open-source product" (for more example, see Table 2.1). Overall, the common characteristic of digital social innovations relies on the ability to tackle social problems such as inequality, social exclusion, poverty, racism, marginalisation and so on. (Bhatt et al., 2019; Hota & Mitra, 2021; Berzin et al., 2018; Qureshi et al., 2018).

This has also stimulated corporations to launch new social programmes to support social entrepreneurs. For instance, Caremakers Invest as recognised to be a Social Solidarity Economy Company (ESUS)

Table 2.1 Examples of Digital Social Innovations. Created by the Author

Company	*Digital Social Innovation Description*	*Country*	*References*
• Plume Labs	This innovation consists in the use of portable sensors to evaluate air pollution and disseminate information through the community. This aims to spread knowledge about the level of pollution and take actions against it from the bottom	France	https://plumelabs.com/en/
• Fairphone	This innovation relies on ethical manufacturing and decent working practices and location in order to produce socially responsible smartphones	Netherlands	https://www.fairphone.com/nl
• Ushahidi	This is a platform that empower citizens and encourage them to develop new solutions for the community	Kenia	https://www.ushahidi.com/
• Safecast	This is an innovation that helps citizens to measure the level of radiation by the use of open hardware and share data	Japan	https://safecast.org/
• Myagro	This innovation was born from the partnership with the corporate company Bayer. Their aim is to support African smallholder farmers and their family to live better and improve their harvest	Africa	https://www.myagro.org/
• Connect Employment Shuttles	This innovation combines innovation and employment. It offers a free training programme for employees and entrepreneurs through online courses	Spain	https://en.fundaciontelefonica.com/employability/lanzaderas-conecta-empleo/

founded by Renault group support economically social entrepreneurs. Tik Tok is dedicated to a section of its platform for social entrepreneurs to enhance the digital inclusive economy. Microsoft supports social entrepreneurs who are making a real impact on society and the environment. Ikea has developed a unit on sustainability that refers to making partnerships with social entrepreneurs for a better inclusive and fair future. In turn, digital social innovations are generated considering the sustainable development goals (SDGs) that induce the involvement of cross-sector collaborations with a different range of stakeholders. This form of innovation is mainly led by social entrepreneurs but they also request the involvement of the ecosystem's actors. Bailey and Lumpkin (2023) introduce the civic wealth creation model to understand the role of different actors in generating civic wealth because those actors are driven by the same interests. They identify three categories of actors such as communities, regimes of support, and enterprises. Each of them brings economic, social, and communal wealth benefits for the community in order to create the blended social value (i.e. a combination of economic and social value).

One of the major issues to overcome for a digital social innovation is the digital gap. Yet, this innovation relies on the adoption of new technologies but not everyone is able to access and \or to use it. Therefore, initially it is necessary to guarantee access to technologies (Qureshi et al., 2018; Riaz & Qureshi, 2017). In this perspective, the European Commission offers several supports; for instance, it has released the European social fund plus (ESF+) to co-finance up-skilling training programmes so as to include marginalised groups of people and help social enterprises. The scope is to offer new digital competencies to foster social inclusion.

The social approach is implemented to prioritise society's challenges. It involves a collaborative approach so as to offer scalable solutions and augment the social impact. Digital social innovation should be in line with three main principles: (1) Technoficing; (2) Satisficing; (3) Socialficing. Technoficing means an appropriate technology is selected to achieve a social goal. Satisficing regards the cognitive limits of a decision maker in individuating and selecting the right solutions (Simon, 1957, 1979); (3) Socialficing concerns getting financial stability in achieving social goals. (Kistruck et al., 2013). Alongside, another leverage is culture. A digital social innovation tends to be originated and implemented in a multicultural context. In turn, a combination of cultural resources become relevant to offer new possibilities. Parthiban et al. (2020) remark the ability of recombining cultural resources to generate a digital social innovation. It calls for cultural bricolage that is widely studied in grassroots communities and refugee entrepreneurship (Baker & Nelson, 2005; Vedula et al., 2022; Abebe, 2023).

Adapting the theoretical model of Montanari et al. (2017) to the current digital social innovation, it is possible to employ their six b*uilding blocks to explore digital social innovations: The first step includes social orientation towards disadvantaged groups of people such as* youth, women, migrants, elderly. In this sense, innovation bridges the welfare state gap trying to solve their social needs. The second step is to offer a novel idea by an open innovation approach that involves the use of advanced technologies. This idea is led by a social mission that includes inclusiveness, social cohesion, equality, and community empowerment. The social mission is a collective input that should generate measurable outputs and social impacts. Third, digital social innovation goes beyond existing space and time boundaries and encourages a participatory approach towards a cross-fertilisation model. It relies on transparency, traceability, and evaluation dimensions to validate the sustainability of such innovations. Fourth, the process of digital social innovation starts from a standard innovation, delivering a prototype and then goes beyond providing a massive dissemination and scalability. Its success regards the strategic alliances and partnership that are developed with and for the local community. Fifth, the governance is multivariate and culturally diverse. It includes different perspectives from different social classes and institutions. Horizontal and collaborative networks are crucial and are empowered by the use of new technologies. Sixth, digital social innovation is influenced by ecosystem dimensions, composed of enabling spaces, financial support, dedicated policies, and incubation hubs. Overall, if social innovation is already relying on a collaborative but local community and approach; digital social innovation goes beyond and integrates the global community via a participatory approach.

Scalability of Digital Social Innovations

As said, digital social innovation needs to be scalable. These features of digital social entrepreneurship as well as digital social innovation will be also discussed in Chapter 5. The concept of scalability is explicated by three functions scaling up, scaling out, and scaling deep. Scaling up refers to the capacity of a digital social innovation to extend the beneficiary served. It needs the support of intermediaries to achieve social goals (Hernberg & Hyysalo, 2024). Scaling out regards the ability to expand the digital social innovation in other territories, increasing the level of social impact. Then, scaling deep concerns improves the impact in the local community. Additionally, the entrepreneurial literature has also identified other forms of scaling: scaling diversification refers to the possibility to use the same platforms to satisfy different SDGs. Scaling across is also recognised as "growing the idea" that adopts the "open innovation approach that focuses on disseminating and sharing the DSI with other DSIs to let the idea grow and, by extension, lead to a higher social impact". (Quereshi et al., 2018, p. 657). The last two are ecosystem approach and scaling by bridging complementary institutional voids. The ecosystem approach remarks that SDGs are wicked problems and cannot be achieved by a single entrepreneur (Bhatt, 2022). This approach highlights the empowerment of a collaborative approach to solve problems. Scaling by bridging complementary institutional voids refers to the individuation of two SDGs to be sorted out contemporary. An example comes from a work of Parthiban et al. (2020), the authors describe that elderly people were teaching poor students in rural areas by a platform that was able to offer a decent work. In this way, the SDG 8 – decent work and economic growth- and the SDG 4 – quality education- are addressed (see Table 2.2).

Table 2.2 Scaling Practices

Scaling Practices	*Description*	*References*
Scaling up	It refers to the capacity of a digital social innovation to extend the beneficiary served. It needs the support of intermediaries to achieve social goals. It aims to "influence on public discourses, political agendas and legislation"	Hernberg and Hyysalo (2024), van Lunenburg et al. (2020)
Scaling out	It regards the extension in other geographic areas	Westley et al. (2014), Hermans et al. (2016)
Scaling deep	It means "focusing…energies and resources on achieving greater impact in your home community by doing one of the following: improving the quality of your services, achieving greater penetration of your target client population, finding new ways to serve your clients, extending your client services to new client groups developing innovative financial management approaches and serving as an example to others in your field"	Eiselein & Dentchev (2021), Taylor et al. (2002, p. 243); Smith & Stevens (2010)
Scaling Diversification	In the context of digital social innovation, it refers to the possibility to use the same platforms for different SDGs	Qureshi et al. (2021)

(*Continued*)

Table 2.2 (continued)

Scaling Practices	*Description*	*References*
Scaling across	It concerns the adoption of the "open innovation approach that focuses on disseminating and sharing the DSI with other DSIs to let the idea grow and, by extension, lead to a higher social impact"	Qureshi et al. (2018, p. 657)
Ecosystem approach	It remarks the power of the collaborative and collective approach to achieve SDGs. This calls for a value co-creation and cross-sector partnerships	Bhatt, (2022), Ostertag et al. (2021), Parthiban et al. (2021)
Scaling by bridging complementary institutional voids	This occurs in context when institutional regulations and support are missing. This is also the case of refugee entrepreneurship	Parthiban et al. (2020), Nason and Bothello (2023)

In doing so, the ecosystem becomes the central leverage in the realisation and implementation of a digital social innovation. Grimes et al. (2020) remark the relevance of scaling impact in achieving sustainable goals even if sometimes companies tend to be too much focused on the scalability rather than on the social mission and impact (Klein et al., 2020; Ometto et al., 2019). Digital social innovations lead to a systemic change to generate a lasting and important impact to not just a local community but also for other territories. This also requests people with ethical and cultural perspectives that englobe differences and divergences. An interrelation of multiple systems of power and social structures is the new setting to generate digital social innovation (Zheng & Walsham, 2021). Thinking of these social structures as generated by institutions would be time consuming. Yet, the bottom-up cooperation will be the right approach to include the whole community and generale social inclusion and cohesion. Inclusivity and social cohesion are the glue of the community. This reduces the level of opportunism and allows the capitalism of altruism à la Collier (2019).

Conclusion

Some scholars raise important critical questions regarding the nature and effects of social innovation, especially when it is expressed through digital tools and languages. Nicholls and Murdock (2012) warn against the risk that discourse on social innovation might be "captured" by neoliberal logics, where concepts such as efficiency, impact measurability, and economic sustainability tend to supplant the transformative and political dimension of social action. In this perspective, innovation risks being reduced to a managerial technique, rather than a critical process capable of questioning the status quo. Laville and Eynaud (2019) remark that social innovation cannot be exhausted in procedural or technological solutions. True social innovation, according to the authors, is such only if it is capable of redefining power relations, expanding the boundaries of social inclusion, and promoting new forms of active and democratic citizenship. In a nutshell, innovation cannot be understood as simple functional adaptation to new needs, but must generate epistemological and institutional ruptures capable of producing greater equity and participation. The risk is that digital tools and efficiency-oriented models end up prevailing over values of inclusion, participation, and social justice. In these cases, innovation can transform into a functional exercise, which privileges what is easily measurable, neglecting instead deeper cultural and relational change. To avoid this risk, it is essential that DSE be guided by clear values and conscious vision, capable of using technology not as an end, but as a tool to generate equitable and lasting impact.

In summary, the evolution from Schumpeter to social enterprise – and then to Digital Social Entrepreneurship – shows a process of adaptation and overcoming of the original paradigm. Whilst the Schumpeterian entrepreneur acts to generate profit through innovation, the digital social entrepreneur acts to generate social impact through networks, technologies, and collaboration. In this new model, innovation does not only destroy to create new economic value, but transforms to build relationships, abilities, and inclusion. A la Schumpeter, the digital social entrepreneur is not simply a subject who manages an economic activity, but one who introduces "new combinations" of productive factors, breaking with routines and existing equilibria. This act of disruption represents the essence of economic development, which is not a linear or incremental process, but the result of sudden and discontinuous changes. These innovations do not necessarily have to derive from scientific discoveries or technological inventions (Box 2.1). The entrepreneur is not necessarily an inventor, but is one who recognises innovative potential and translates it into economic practice, taking on the risks of uncertainty and guiding transformation. In this sense, the Schumpeterian entrepreneur is first and foremost a visionary, an agent of change who breaks equilibrium to generate a new trajectory of development. His vision can be integrated in the modern situation of the social entrepreneur who acts in the digital age, promoting solutions that generate inclusion, justice, and participation.

Box 2.1 Case Study

The Forword Team: Where Skills Meet Creativity, inclusivity and Innovation

> "Take care of the sense, and the sounds will take care of themselves"
>
> – *Lewis Carroll, Through the Looking-Glass*, 1871

Forword is an association of professional business women specialising in content accessibility.

Founded in 2011, the project is based in Turin but operates across Italy. It was established to combine the linguistic and organisational skills of the three founding members: Alice Catalano, Marta Bressello, and Silvia Scarpitti (see Figure 2.1 and Figure 2.2).

The legal structure of the association allowed them to diverge from the standard dynamics of the audiovisual industry, which is largely dominated by freelancers working directly with dubbing companies or production houses.

They provide "subtitling for deaf and hard-of-hearing audiences and audio description for blind and visually impaired people".

Figure 2.1 The founders. Photograph by The Founders.

Figure 2.2 The logo. Photograph by The Founders.

They also offer tailor made courses in audio description, interlingual and intralingual subtitling.

From the outset, their goal was to offer a more comprehensive service to end clients, supported by a larger and more structured team capable of handling high volumes of work and involving additional external professionals.

From the beginning, Forword has believed in teamwork. Thanks to a network of trusted collaborators – many of whom were trained by the founders themselves through their teaching roles in Italian universities and Master's programmes – Forword is able to manage large-scale projects and make content accessible to international markets through native-speaking professionals.

A Mission Rooted in Inclusion

The founding partners aimed to carve out a significant market share and establish themselves in terms of both quality and quantity. Their goal was to be recognised nationally as a provider of audiovisual translation services.

Forword has been operating for 15 years in the field of audiovisual and textual translation, with a strong focus on accessibility services – processes that make content usable by individuals with sensory or cognitive disabilities, thus promoting a culture of inclusivity.

"Accessibility" refers to any creative adaptation that meets the needs of sensory-impaired individuals (deaf or hard of hearing, blind or visually impaired), enabling them to enjoy films, theatre performances, exhibition content, videos on websites or social media. Although initially designed for sensory-impaired users, these services are also useful for other groups with difficulties: the elderly, children, foreign language speakers, people on the autism spectrum, and individuals with dyslexia. Each Forword project follows the innovative principles of "Design for All": Everything that is designed and produced must be accessible, easy to use, and responsive to the evolving nature of human diversity, in order to promote equal opportunities for participation in all areas of society.

Forword is also an associate partner in the Erasmus+ project Train2Validate, which promotes global best practices in Easy to Read (E2R) writing and is a partner of SELLA Innovation Lab.

Whatever the service, the ultimate goal is to create fully accessible, 360-degree projects that involve professionals from across the audiovisual sector and trade associations, promoting initiatives with a tangible social impact.

Some of Forword projects are outlined as follows.

Forword makes film and audiovisual content accessible for production and post- production companies that benefit from Tax Credit incentives and are therefore required to produce audio descriptions for blind individuals and subtitles for deaf individuals, in compliance with Law 228 on the regulation of cinema and audiovisual media.

Years of activity: 2015 – ongoing

Forword provides audio descriptions for major titles produced by Apple TV+, Disney, Warner Brothers, Prime Video and other major streaming platforms.

Years of activity: 2019 – ongoing

Forword offers accessibility consulting services to institutions, production companies, theatres, and museums – developing the most appropriate solutions for each case. This may include designing an accessible path for an exhibition, creating accessible promotional videos or audio guide content for a museum, or making theatre performances, live events, and even podcasts accessible.

Years of activity: 2015 – ongoing

Social Impact and Vision

Over the past 15 years, the Italian audiovisual distribution market has undergone significant changes in terms of accessibility. Forword has gradually positioned itself as a key player in the sector, diversifying its services while always keeping social impact at the forefront: accessible products are the most inclusive on the market, reaching all types of audiences and ensuring a uniform experience across ages, disabilities, and linguistic backgrounds. Breaking down cultural barriers has always been a core value for the association and remains the primary benchmark in evaluating projects and client requests.

Forword has also invested significant energy in training a new generation of professionals who are aware, sensitive to inclusion, and equipped with a strong work ethic. The founding partners believe that having skilled audiovisual professionals in the market – who share these values and apply them in their daily work – adds value to the entire industry.

References

Abebe, S. A. (2023). Refugee entrepreneurship: systematic and thematic analyses and a research agenda. *Small Business Economics*, 60(1), 315–350.

Bacq, S., & Eddleston, K. A. (2018). A resource-based view of social entrepreneurship: How stewardship culture benefits scale of social impact. *Journal of Business Ethics*, 152, 589–611.

Bacq, S., & Janssen, F. (2011). The multiple faces of social entrepreneurship: A review of definitional issues based on geographical and thematic criteria. *Entrepreneurship & Regional Development*, 23(5–6), 373–403.

Bailey, R. C., & Lumpkin, G. T. (2023). Enacting positive social change: A civic wealth creation stakeholder engagement framework. *Entrepreneurship Theory and Practice*, 47(1), 66–90.

Baker, T., & Nelson, R. E. (2005). Creating something from nothing: Resource construction through entrepreneurial bricolage. *Administrative Science Quarterly*, 50(3), 329–366.

Berzin, S. C., Lee, H., & Leong, A. D. (2018). Social entrepreneurship as intervention: Findings from a venture development program for marginalized youth. *Child & Youth Services*, 39(4), 211–227.

Bhatt, B. (2022). Ethical complexity of social change: Negotiated actions of a social enterprise. *Journal of Business Ethics*, 177(4), 743–762.

Bhatt, B., Qureshi, I., & Riaz, S. (2019). Social entrepreneurship in non-munificent institutional environments and implications for institutional work: Insights from China. *Journal of Business Ethics*, 154, 605–630.

Charalabidis, Y., N. Loukis, Androutsopoulou, A. Karkaletsis, V. & Triantafillou, A. (2014). Passive crowdsourcing in government using social media. *Transforming Government: People, Process and Policy*, 8(2), 283–308.

Chesbrough, H., Vanhaverbeke, W., & West, J. (Eds.). (2014). *New frontiers in open innovation*. Oxford: OUP.

Collier, P. (2019). *The Future of Capitalism: Facing the New Anxieties*. UK: Allen Lane- Penguin Books.

Croitoru, A. (2019). No entrepreneurship without opportunity: The intersection of return migration research and entrepreneurship literature. *Social Change Review*, *17*(Winter), 33–60.

Drucker, P. F. (2002). The discipline of innovation. *Harvard Business Review*, 80(8), 95–102.

Edwards-Schachter, M., & Wallace, M. L. (2017). "Shaken, but not stirred": Sixty years of defining social innovation. *Technological Forecasting and Social Change*, 119, 64–79.

Eiselein, P., & Dentchev, N. A. (2021). Scaling social impact: What challenges and opportunities await social entrepreneurs. *Social Entrepreneurship*, 5, 145–172.

El-Haddadeh, R., Irani, Z., Millard, J., & Schröder, A. (2014). Toward a coherent methodological framework for examining social innovation in the public sector. *Information Systems Management*, 31(3), 250–258.

European Commission. (2013). Retrieved from https://single-market-economy.ec.europa.eu/industry/strategy/innovation/social_en on 05.01. 2025

Grimes, M. G., Williams, T. A., & Zhao, E. Y. (2020). Beyond hybridity: Accounting for the values complexity of all organizations in the study of mission and mission drift. *Academy of Management Review*, 45(1), 234–238.

Hermans, F., Roep, D., & Klerkx, L. (2016). Scale dynamics of grassroots innovations through parallel pathways of transformative change. *Ecological Economics*, 130, 285–295.

Hernberg, H., & Hyysalo, S. (2024). Modes of intermediation: How intermediaries engage in advancing local bottom-up experimentation. *Environmental Innovation and Societal Transitions*, 51, 100849.

Hota, P. K., & Mitra, S. (2021). Leveraging the power of sharing: The case of a social enterprise at the base of the pyramid. *Sharing Economy at the Base of the Pyramid: Opportunities and Challenges*, 149–171.

Kahn, K. B. (2018). Understanding innovation. *Business Horizons*, 61(3), 453–460.

Kistruck, G. M., Beamish, P. W., Qureshi, I., & Sutter, C. J. (2013). Social intermediation in base-of-the-pyramid markets. *Journal of Management Studies*, 50(1), 31–66.

Klein, S., Schneider, S., & Spieth, P. (2020). How to stay on the road? A business model perspective on mission drift in social purpose organizations. *Journal of Business Research*, 125, 658–671. https://doi.org/10.1016/j.jbusres.2020.01.053

Laville, J. L., & Eynaud, P. (2019). Rethinking social enterprise through philanthropic and democratic solidarities. In *Theory of Social Enterprise and Pluralism* (pp. 18–43). Routledge.

Montanari, F., Sgaragli, F., & Teloni, D. (2017). Le dimensioni dell'innovazione sociale per il design e l'implementazione di politiche pubbliche efficaci. *Impresa sociale*, (10).

Murray, R., Caulier-Grice, J., & Mulgan, G. (2010). *The Open Book of Social Innovation* (Vol. 24). London: Nesta.

Nason, R., & Bothello, J. (2023). Far from void: How institutions shape growth in informal economies. *Academy of Management Review*, 48(3), 485–503.

Nicholls, A., & Murdock, A. (2012). The nature of social innovation. In *Social innovation: Blurring Boundaries to Reconfigure Markets* (pp. 1–30). London: Springer Link, Palgrave Macmillan UK.

Ometto, M. P., Gegenhuber, T., Winter, J., & Greenwood, R. (2019). From balancing missions to mission drift: The role of the institutional context, spaces, and compartmentalization in the scaling of social enterprises. *Business & Society*, 58(5), 1003–1046.

Ostertag, F., Hahn, R., & Ince, I. (2021). Blended value co-creation: A qualitative investigation of relationship designs of social enterprises. *Journal of Business Research*, 129, 428–445.

Parthiban, R., Qureshi, I., Bandyopadhyay, S., Bhatt, B., & Jaikumar, S. (2020). Leveraging ICT to overcome complementary institutional voids: Insights from institutional work by a social enterprise to help marginalized. *Information Systems Frontiers*, 22(11), 1–21. https://doi.org/10.1007/s10796-020-09991-6

Parthiban, R., Qureshi, I., Bandyopadhyay, S., & Jaikumar, S. (2021). Digitally mediated value creation for non-commodity base of the pyramid producers. *International Journal of Information Management*, 56(2021), 1–17.

Phillips, W., Lee, H., Ghobadian, A., O'Regan, N., & James, P. (2015). Social innovation and social entrepreneurship: A systematic review. *Group & Organization Management*, 40(3), 428–461.

Phills J.A., Deiglmeier K., Miller D.T. (2008). Rediscovering social innovation. *Stanford Social Innovation Review*, 6(4), 34–43.

Qureshi, I., Pan, S. L., & Zheng, Y. (2021). Digital social innovation: An overview and research framework. *Information Systems Journal*, 31(5), 647–671.

Qureshi, I., Sutter, C., & Bhatt, B. (2018). The transformative power of knowledge sharing in settings of poverty and social inequality. *Organization Studies*, 39(11), 1575–1599.

Ramani, S. V., SadreGhazi, S., & Gupta, S. (2017). Catalysing innovation for social impact: The role of social enterprises in the Indian sanitation sector. *Technological Forecasting and Social Change*, 121, 216–227.

Riaz, S., & Qureshi, I. (2017). Emergence of a new institutional logic: Shaping the institutionally complex field of community radio in India. In *Emergence* (Vol. 50, pp. 383–418). Emerald Publishing Limited, Bradford, UK.

Schumpeter, T. (1934) *The Theory of Economic Development*. Cambridge, MA: Harvard University.

Shalini, R., Selvamani, L., Lal, S. R., & Lakshmi, G. D. (2025, March). Assessing students' perception towards metaverse technology: A study on the social sustainability of immersive virtual technologies in higher educational institutions. In *2025 International Conference on Computing for Sustainability and Intelligent Future (COMP-SIF)* (pp. 1–6). IEEE.

Simon, H. (1957). The compensation of executives. *Sociometry*, 20(1), 32–35. https://doi.org/10.2307/2786111

Simon, H. (1979). Rational decision making in business organizations. *American Economic Review*, 69(4), 493–513.

Smith, B. R., & Stevens, C. E. (2010). Different types of social entrepreneurship: The role of geography and embeddedness on the measurement and scaling of social value. *Entrepreneurship & Regional Development*, 22(6), 575–598.

Taylor, M. A., Dees, J. G., & Emerson, J. (2002). The question of scale: Finding an appropriate strategy for building on your success. *Strategic Tools for Social Entrepreneurs: Enhancing the Performance of Your Enterprising Nonprofit*, 235–266. In Dees, J. G., Emerson, J., & Economy, P. (2004). Strategic tools for social entrepreneurs: Enhancing the performance of your enterprising nonprofit. John Wiley & Sons, New York, USA.

Tracey, P., & Stott, N. (2017). Social innovation: A window on alternative ways of organizing and innovating. *Innovation*, 19(1), 51–60.

Van der Have, R. P., & Rubalcaba, L. (2016). Social innovation research: An emerging area of innovation studies? *Research Policy*, 45(9), 1923–1935.

van Lunenburg, M., Geuijen, K., & Meijer, A. (2020). How and why do social and sustainable initiatives scale? A systematic review of the literature on social entrepreneurship and grassroots innovation. *VOLUNTAS: International Journal of Voluntary and Nonprofit Organizations*, 31(5), 1013–1024.

Westley, F., Antadze, N., Riddell, D. J., Robinson, K., & Geobey, S. (2014). Five configurations for scaling up social innovation: Case examples of nonprofit organizations from Canada. *Journal of Applied Behavioral Science*, 50, 234–260.

Zheng, Y., & Walsham, G. (2021). Inequality of what? An intersectional approach to digital inequality under Covid-19. *Information and Organization*, 31(1), 100341.

3 A New Virtual Scenario

Artificial Intelligence, Metaverse, and Augmented Reality for Digital Social Enterprises

Theofilos Tzanidis

Introduction and Conceptual Framework

The landscape of social entrepreneurship is evolving significantly due to the integration of digital technologies, transitioning from traditional community-based models to sophisticated digital social enterprises (DSEs) that utilise technological advancements to address complex societal issues. These DSEs represent a hybrid organisational form, merging the social mission focus of traditional social enterprises with the efficiency and scalability provided by digital technologies. The applicability of technologies such as artificial intelligence (AI) and augmented reality (AR) is becoming increasingly critical in this transformation, enhancing the operational capabilities and potential social impacts of these enterprises (Wales & Gupta, 2020; Nair, 2022).

The integration of AI within DSEs exemplifies this transformation, enhancing operational efficiency and effectiveness. By utilising intelligent data processing, predictive analytics, and automated decision-making capabilities, DSEs can deliver personalised services at scale Giderler & Vanclay, 2024; Iskandar et al., 2021). The role of AI extends beyond mere operational improvements, enabling social enterprises to develop tailored community solutions dynamically based on real-time data, ultimately augmenting their social impact (Wales & Gupta, 2020; Giderler & Vanclay, 2024).

Augmented reality technologies bridge physical and digital interactions to enrich real-world experiences, allowing DSEs to create engaging educational content and improve community intervention approaches (Nair, 2022; Giderler & Vanclay, 2024). Furthermore, the metaverse represents a revolutionary development in social interaction and economic engagement, providing immersive environments where DSEs can innovate their service delivery models, fostering community building and establishing novel revenue streams through virtual engagements (Kusumawardani et al., 2024; Youssef et al., 2024).

DOI: 10.4324/9781003583448-4

The framework of impact amplification reflects how the synergies created through the convergence of AI and AR technologies can exceed individual contributions to the operations and mission fulfilment of social enterprises. This synergy reflects a broader understanding of DSEs operating within complex ecosystems of multiple stakeholders, necessitating a shift from traditional linear models of social impact measurement (Urmanavičienė, 2020; Palil et al., 2023). The requirement for a more integrative approach acknowledges the interconnected challenges faced today, thus propelling the need for social enterprises that utilise technological ingenuity to foster systemic social value (Emmanuel et al., 2024).

Moreover, the incorporation of these technologies fundamentally changes the traditional metrics of success that social enterprises have long relied upon. As the lines between profit motives and social objectives blur, continuous assessment of social impacts becomes crucial. DSEs must now navigate new models of impact assessment that extend beyond basic financial considerations to include social return on investment (SROI), leveraging data and performance metrics that reflect both economic viability and significant social outcomes (Iskandar et al., 2021; Thomas, 2019). This holistic perspective is essential for ensuring the sustainability and growth of social enterprises in the evolving digital landscape.

The transformation of social entrepreneurship through digital technologies not only enhances operational capabilities but also enables new paradigms of social engagement and impact assessment. By integrating AI and AR, DSEs can cultivate more meaningful connections with their communities while addressing complex social challenges with innovative solutions.

Market Context and Growth Projections

The technological landscape presents extraordinary growth trajectories that underscore the strategic importance of early adoption for social enterprises. The global metaverse market, valued at £737.73 billion in 2024, is projected to reach £7.64 trillion by 2032, representing a compound annual growth rate of 29.2% (Fortune Business Insights, 2024). Similarly, the augmented reality market demonstrates remarkable expansion potential, growing from £29.6 billion in 2024 to an anticipated £591.7 billion by 2033 – a staggering 39.5% CAGR (Market Scoop, 2025 see Table 3.1).

However, these impressive global statistics contrast sharply with adoption rates within the social enterprise sector. Current research reveals that only 11% of European social enterprises consider AI and machine learning relevant to their operations, compared to 78% of general organisations

Table 3.1 Technology Market Growth Projections. Various Industry Reports, 2024–2025

Technology	*2024 Market Value*	*2032/2033 Projection*	*CAGR*
AI global market	£279.22 billion	£1,811.75 billion	35.9%
Metaverse	£737.73 billion	£7.64 trillion	29.2%
Augmented reality	£29.6 billion	£591.7 billion	39.5%

using AI in at least one business function (Statista, 2024; McKinsey & Company, 2024). This disparity represents both a significant challenge and an extraordinary opportunity for the sector.

The percentage of social challenges is increasing in the UK. For instance, the number of young people who were not in education, employment or training (NEET) has grown, requesting more support from the government. "This is up 1.3 percentage points, compared with October to December 2023, and up 0.3 percentage points on the previous quarter". (Office for National Statistics, 2025). However, public interventions are not enough to solve social problems. Social enterprises assume a crucial role in offering high-quality public services. They are a vital part of the welfare system. This has triggered the growth of these enterprises. Recent government research identifies 471,000 social enterprises operating across the United Kingdom, comprising approximately 9% of the small business population (Civil Society, 2024). These organisations collectively employ 2.3 million people and generate £1.2 billion in annual profit, demonstrating substantial economic significance alongside their social mission focus (Social Enterprise UK, 2024).

The sector exhibits characteristics particularly conducive to technology adoption: 85.5% of social enterprises are founded on innovative approaches, significantly higher than traditional SMEs, and they demonstrate superior employment practices with 84% paying the Living Wage compared to lower rates in conventional sectors (Social Enterprise UK, 2024, see Figure 3.1). Furthermore, 22% are in the most deprived areas compared to 14% of general businesses, positioning them strategically to address digital exclusion whilst leveraging technology for enhanced service delivery.

Investment flows into the sector have shown remarkable growth, with social investments increasing from £830 million in 2021 to over £10 billion in 2023. The Social Investment Tax Relief (SITR) scheme has facilitated £5.4 million in investments across 40 enterprises, whilst the Enterprise Investment Scheme raised £1.575 billion for 3,780 companies in 2023–2024 (HM Government, 2025). This growing financial ecosystem provides the foundation necessary for technology adoption and scaling.

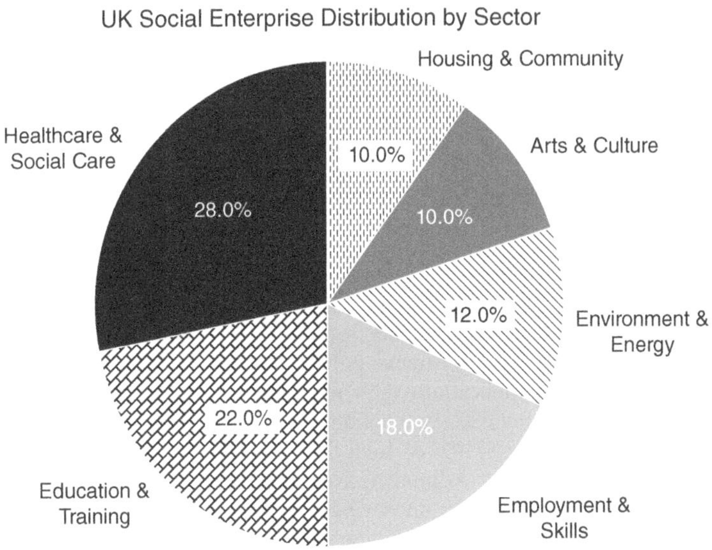

Figure 3.1 UK social enterprise sector distribution. Adapted from Social Enterprise UK, 2024.

Artificial Intelligence in Digital Social Enterprises

The artificial intelligence market has experienced exponential growth, with global market size valued at £279.22 billion in 2024 and projected to reach £1.81 trillion by 2030, representing a compound annual growth rate of 35.9% (Grand View Research, 2024). This remarkable expansion reflects the technology's maturation and increasing recognition of its transformative potential across diverse sectors, including social enterprise applications. North America currently dominates the AI market, accounting for over 29.5% of global revenue in 2024, driven by favourable government initiatives and robust technological infrastructure.

The adoption patterns within the social enterprise sector reveal significant momentum, with almost half of UK social enterprises reporting some form of AI utilisation according to recent research (Hall & Alexander, 2023). This adoption rate demonstrates the sector's proactive engagement with emerging technologies, despite the resource constraints typically associated with social enterprise operations. The most adopted AI applications among social enterprises include text generation using large language models, utilised by 17% of surveyed organisations, and visual content creation and data processing through machine learning, each employed by 10% of the sample.

Table 3.2 AI Implementation Economics for Social Enterprises. Multiple industry Reports, 2024

Application Area	*Cost Reduction*	*Implementation Cost*	*Payback Period*
Administrative automation	20–30%	£50,000–£200,000	12–18 months
Content creation	40–60%	£25,000–£100,000	6–12 months
Data analysis & insights	50–70%	£100,000–£500,000	18–24 months
Customer service	25–35%	£75,000–£300,000	12–24 months

Quantifiable economic benefits from AI implementation demonstrate substantial return on investment potential across multiple application areas. Healthcare applications show particularly strong economics, with AI potentially saving £200–360 billion annually in systems like the NHS alone – representing 5–10% of total healthcare spending (University of North Carolina, 2024). Administrative automation consistently delivers 20% cost reductions whilst improving service quality, with documented examples including Netflix's £1 billion annual savings from AI recommendation systems.

The research reveals specific cost-benefit ratios that social enterprises can anticipate. See Table 3.2.

The implementation of AI technologies in social enterprise operations encompasses diverse applications that span administrative functions, service delivery, and impact measurement. Generative AI has emerged as a transformative tool that can function as a highly effective assistant for social enterprises, automating tasks such as content creation, brief drafting, and impact report generation (SEWF Online, 2024). This automation capability enables social enterprises to redirect human resources towards core mission activities whilst maintaining high standards of documentation and communication. Content creation represents one of the most immediately accessible AI applications for social enterprises. Large language models can generate marketing materials, social media content, grant proposals, and educational resources, significantly reducing the time and expertise requirements traditionally associated with these tasks. This capability is particularly valuable for smaller social enterprises that may lack dedicated marketing or communications staff but require professional-quality content to effectively communicate their mission and impact to stakeholders.

Case Study: Ashoka's AI Transformation

Ashoka, the global network of social entrepreneurs, exemplifies successful AI implementation within the social sector. Partnership with technology company "Tooploox" created a sophisticated semantic database processing over 20,000 pages of organisational data. The AI-powered system eliminated information bottlenecks and enabled staff across 30 countries to access specialist knowledge efficiently. This transformation reduced research time by 75% whilst improving the quality of entrepreneur matching and programme recommendations (MovingWorlds, 2024).

Data processing and analysis constitute another critical area where AI technologies provide substantial value to social enterprises. Machine learning algorithms can analyse complex datasets to identify patterns, predict outcomes, and optimise resource allocation. For social enterprises working in areas such as poverty alleviation, education, or healthcare, this analytical capability can enhance programme effectiveness by identifying the most impactful interventions and optimising service delivery approaches.

Impact Measurement and Evidence Generation

The integration of AI in impact measurement represents a significant development for social enterprises, which traditionally face challenges in demonstrating and quantifying their social impact Lévesque et al. (2020). AI-powered analytics have the capability to process diverse data sources, including social media sentiment, survey responses, and behavioural indicators. This allows social enterprises to provide comprehensive impact assessments that satisfy stakeholder requirements while also informing programme improvements (Ali, 2024). Specifically, AI can discern patterns and insights from large datasets, enabling organisations to better understand the effectiveness of their initiatives and adapt strategies accordingly (Zhou & Cen, 2024). Empirical research demonstrates positive correlations between AI integration and organisational performance in social enterprise contexts. For instance, a study examining digital leadership found that AI technologies enhance the effectiveness of leadership practices through improved decision-making and resource allocation (Lin, 2023). The presence of AI facilitates enhanced customer interaction, thus transforming traditional leadership dynamics within social enterprises. Consequently, this integration supports innovative practices within these organisations, contributing to a culture of continuous improvement and adaptability to evolving challenges (Yasni et al., 2023). The effective integration of AI technologies into impact measurement frameworks is crucial for social enterprises. Not only does it enhance their ability to demonstrate social value, but it also empowers leadership and fosters innovation, thereby fortifying the enterprise's position within the socio-economic ecosystem (Huruta et al., 2020) (Figure 3.2).

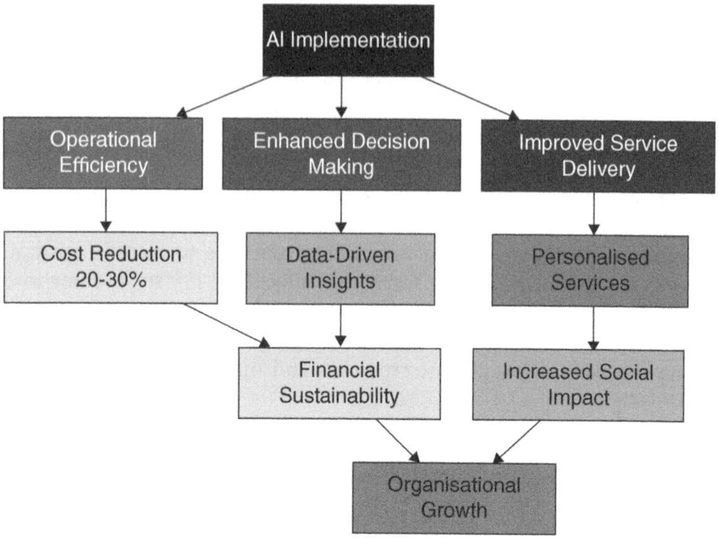

Figure 3.2 AI impact pathway for social enterprises. Created by the Author.

Metaverse as a Platform for Social Innovation

The metaverse industry represents one of the fastest-growing technological sectors, with market valuation reaching £146.6 billion in 2024 and projections indicating growth to £1.1 trillion by 2030, representing a compound annual growth rate of 39.3% (Globe Newswire, 2025). This extraordinary growth trajectory reflects the convergence of multiple technological advances, including virtual reality, augmented reality, blockchain technology, and high-speed internet infrastructure, creating an ecosystem capable of supporting persistent, immersive virtual environments.

Investment patterns within the metaverse sector demonstrate significant commitment from both technology giants and emerging startups, driving innovation and expanding platform capabilities (Jauhiainen et al., 2022; Huynh-The et al., 2023). This investment environment creates opportunities for social enterprises to access sophisticated technological infrastructure without necessitating substantial upfront capital investments, as many metaverse platforms operate on service-based or revenue-sharing models (Omrani et al., 2024; Zhong & Zhao, 2024). Such models enable social enterprises to leverage advanced technologies – like virtual reality (VR) and augmented reality (AR) – effectively while minimising financial barriers associated with traditional technology adoption (Gil-Cordero et al., 2023).

The geographic distribution of metaverse development and adoption reveals important considerations for social enterprises operating in varying regional contexts. North America and Asia-Pacific currently dominate market activity, but emerging markets are experiencing rapid adoption rates (Bartoli et al., 2024). This trend creates opportunities for social enterprises to capitalise on metaverse technologies for community development and social impact initiatives, particularly in underserved regions (Bartoli et al., 2024). In these contexts, the potential for metaverse applications to facilitate social interactions and provide immersive experiences becomes particularly beneficial, enabling organisations to engage with communities in novel ways (Tunca et al., 2023). Therefore, as the metaverse continues to evolve, social enterprises can strategically position themselves to harness these technologies for broader social good (Duan et al., 2021). The intersection of investment, technological infrastructure, and geographic considerations within the metaverse provides a fertile ground for social enterprise expansion and innovation across various global contexts.

The metaverse's capacity for social impact derives from its fundamental characteristics as a platform that transcends geographical barriers, enables scalable virtual interactions, and creates new forms of economic activity. Digital socialisation capabilities allow people from diverse backgrounds to interact, collaborate, and socialise in common virtual spaces, potentially reducing isolation, bridging cultural divides, and fostering international understanding (Top Software Companies, 2024). This capability is particularly relevant for social enterprises working on global challenges that require cross-cultural collaboration and understanding.

Educational applications represent a particularly promising area for social enterprise metaverse utilisation. Virtual classrooms and learning environments can provide access to high-quality educational content regardless of geographical location, addressing educational inequality and expanding learning opportunities for underserved populations. Research by PwC demonstrates that VR training achieves completion rates 4x faster than classroom methods whilst improving confidence levels by 275% (PwC, 2024). Considering young NEET people, this is also an opportunity to enhance their learning journey. If we think that 1999 the Social Exclusion UNIT has delivered a programme to improve quality life for this category of individuals, how would they get benefit through using AI and\or metaverse? The use of these technologies for NEET is still a challenge but the positive feelings encourage their use towards disadvantaged people.

Case Study: ENGAGE XR Platform

ENGAGE XR serves over 200 organisations globally with educational and enterprise metaverse solutions, demonstrating scalable business models for social good applications. The platform's K12 education bundles have enabled schools in remote areas to access specialist teaching and collaborative learning experiences previously unavailable due to geographical constraints. Virtual field trips to historical sites and scientific laboratories have enhanced learning outcomes whilst reducing costs and environmental impact (ENGAGE, 2024).

Healthcare applications within the metaverse offer significant potential for social enterprises focused on health equity and access issues. Virtual healthcare consultations, therapy sessions, and support groups can extend healthcare access to remote or underserved communities whilst reducing costs and improving convenience for patients. Mental health applications particularly benefit from the anonymity and accessibility provided by virtual environments.

In addition to healthcare the above named platform serves as a dynamic platform for a variety of social enterprise activities, leveraging its immersive virtual environments to foster community, education, and professional development. Through virtual events, organisations can host inclusive and accessible gatherings, such as conferences and product launches, breaking down geographical barriers and reducing the carbon footprint associated with travel. The platform's educational capabilities offer significant social value, enabling virtual field trips to historical sites and scientific explorations that might otherwise be inaccessible. Furthermore, Engage VR supports workforce development and collaboration through its enterprise solutions, providing innovative and effective virtual reality and augmented reality training and onboarding, particularly beneficial for remote teams and creating equitable opportunities for skill-building and employment. These features collectively empower social enterprises to deliver impactful experiences that drive positive social change.

Economic Models and Revenue Generation

The metaverse creates multiple economic opportunities for digital social enterprises through new revenue models, market expansion capabilities, and cost reduction potential. Virtual real estate represents an emerging asset class where social enterprises can establish virtual headquarters, community centres, or service delivery facilities without the overhead costs associated with physical locations. This virtual presence can enable social enterprises to expand their geographical reach whilst maintaining a professional organisational presence.

Digital asset creation and management offer revenue generation opportunities through the development and sale of virtual goods, services, and experiences. Social enterprises can create educational content, virtual experiences, or digital tools that generate revenue whilst advancing their social mission. The creator economy within metaverse platforms enables social enterprises to monetise their expertise and content whilst building sustainable revenue streams (Table 3.3).

Table 3.3 Metaverse Revenue Models for Social Enterprises. Industry Analysis, 2024

Revenue Model	*Implementation Cost*	*Potential Annual Revenue*	*Time to Market*
Virtual Events	£25,000–£100,000	£100,000–£500,000	3–6 months
Educational Content	£50,000–£200,000	£200,000–£1,000,000	6–12 months
Virtual Real Estate	£100,000–£500,000	£150,000–£750,000	12–18 months
Digital Services	£75,000–£300,000	£300,000–£1,500,000	9–15 months

Augmented Reality: Bridging Physical and Digital Social Impact

The augmented reality market has demonstrated substantial growth momentum, with market size valued at £43.4 billion in 2023 and projected to reach £616.84 billion by 2032, growing at a compound annual growth rate of 34.3% (SkyQuest Technology, 2024). This growth reflects increasing recognition of AR's potential to enhance real-world experiences through digital overlay technologies, creating new opportunities for social impact applications.

The adoption patterns within the augmented reality (AR) market reveal significant growth across multiple sectors relevant to social enterprise operations. Healthcare applications are driving substantial adoption, as AR technologies enhance medical training, surgical assistance, and patient education Liu et al. (2024), Riar et al., 2022). The ability of AR to provide immersive experiences enhances the learning and practical application of medical professionals, potentially leading to improved patient care outcomes (Sharma, 2023).

Moreover, the retail and e-commerce sectors are experiencing rapid AR integration, creating models that social enterprises can adapt for their service delivery and revenue generation activities. Retailers utilise AR to refine customer interactions through virtual try-ons and personalised product experiences, demonstrating how social enterprises can leverage similar technologies to engage their target audiences (Liu & Lin, 2022; Abed, 2021). As noted, "AR combines the real and virtual world by superimposing virtual elements into a real-world environment", transforming the consumer shopping experience and providing substantial engagement opportunities (Abed, 2021).

The hardware segment of the AR market is experiencing rapid growth, indicating increasing accessibility and sophistication of AR devices. This trend suggests that AR applications will become more accessible to social enterprise users and beneficiaries, thereby reducing barriers to adoption and enabling more widespread implementation of AR-based social programmes (COVACI et al., 2022; Brown et al., 2024). In particular, the decreasing costs and improving technology of AR devices allow for broader utilisation across various sectors. As AR becomes more embedded within organisational practices in social enterprises, it is likely to support innovative outreach and programming methods, particularly in resource-constrained environments (Han et al., 2023). The expanding AR market across healthcare and retail reinforces the potential for social enterprises to leverage these technologies effectively. As AR technologies continue to evolve, they hold the promise of facilitating enhanced service delivery, community engagement, and educational initiatives within underserved areas.

Augmented reality technologies offer transformative potential for community engagement and development initiatives led by digital social enterprises. Research demonstrates that VR and AR technologies significantly enhance community engagement and participation in social entrepreneurship projects, with social entrepreneurs reporting improved outreach, better visualisation of social issues, and increased empathy among participants (Journal of Social Entrepreneurship Action, 2024).

The visualisation capabilities of AR technology enable social enterprises to make abstract or complex social issues more tangible and understandable for community members and stakeholders. Environmental social enterprises can use AR to visualise pollution levels, climate change impacts, or conservation benefits in real-time, creating more compelling and actionable information for community members. Urban development social enterprises can use AR to show proposed improvements to neighbourhoods, enabling more informed community participation in planning processes.

Case Study: Cultural Heritage Preservation

Backup Ukraine demonstrates innovative AR applications for cultural preservation during crisis situations. The initiative uses community-driven AR scanning to preserve cultural heritage sites during conflict, engaging citizens in preservation efforts whilst creating digital archives for future generations. This approach combines immediate crisis response with long-term cultural preservation, demonstrating AR's potential for social resilience building (Multiple Sources, 2024).

Community mapping and asset identification represent powerful applications of AR technology for social enterprises working in community development. AR applications can overlay information about community resources, services, and opportunities onto real-world environments, helping community members navigate available support systems and identify opportunities for engagement or economic development.

Accessibility and Inclusion Applications

The accessibility implications of AR technology present both opportunities and challenges for social enterprises committed to inclusive service

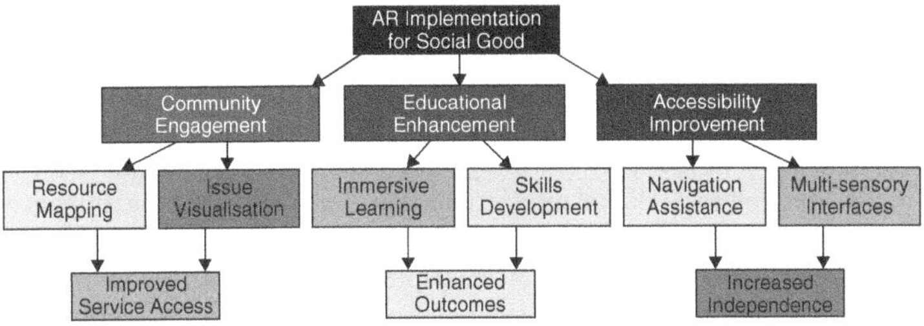

Figure 3.3 AR applications for social enterprise impact.

delivery. Current research reveals that less than 1% of AR research considers disability access, indicating significant development needs for inclusive design (Accessibility.com, 2024). However, innovative applications demonstrate AR's potential to enhance accessibility when designed thoughtfully.

Voice recognition and haptic feedback innovations particularly benefit individuals with mobility challenges, whilst visual AR interfaces can provide navigation assistance for people with visual impairments. Social enterprises can leverage these capabilities to create more inclusive service delivery models that accommodate diverse user needs and preferences (Figure 3.3).

Convergence and Integration: The Triple Technology Framework

The convergence of artificial intelligence, metaverse platforms, and augmented reality technologies creates synergistic effects that exceed the sum of their individual contributions to social enterprise operations. This convergence enables the development of intelligent virtual environments that can adapt to user needs, provide personalised experiences, and optimise social impact delivery through data-driven insights and automated decision-making.

AI serves as the intelligence layer that enhances both metaverse and AR applications through natural language processing, computer vision, predictive analytics, and machine learning capabilities. In metaverse environments, AI enables intelligent virtual assistants, automated content generation, personalised experience delivery, and dynamic environment optimisation based on user behaviour and preferences. For AR applications, AI provides object recognition, contextual information delivery, real-time translation, and adaptive user interface optimisation.

The metaverse provides platform infrastructure that enables scalable deployment of both AI and AR technologies, creating persistent virtual environments where social enterprises can deliver services, build communities, and generate revenue. Within metaverse platforms, AR technologies can enhance virtual experiences by integrating real-world information and enabling hybrid physical-digital interactions that extend the reach and impact of virtual social programmes.

Successful implementation of the triple technology framework requires strategic approaches that consider organisational capacity, community needs, technological infrastructure, and financial sustainability. Social enterprises should adopt phased implementation strategies that begin with single technology applications and gradually integrate additional technologies as capacity and experience develop.

The initial phase should focus on identifying the technology that offers the most immediate value for the organisation's specific social mission and operational context. For social enterprises with strong content creation needs, AI implementation through generative language models may provide immediate efficiency gains and cost reductions. Organisations with geographically dispersed communities might prioritise metaverse platform adoption to enable virtual community building and service delivery (see Table 3.4).

Capacity building represents a critical component of successful implementation, requiring investment in staff training, technology infrastructure, and ongoing technical support. Social enterprises should develop partnerships with technology providers, educational institutions, and other social enterprises to share implementation costs and knowledge whilst building collective capacity for technology adoption.

Table 3.4 Technology Implementation Roadmap for Social Enterprises. Created by the Author

Phase	*Duration*	*Technology Focus*	*Investment Range*	*Expected Outcomes*
1: Foundation	6–12 months	AI automation tools	£25,000–£100,000	20–30% efficiency gains
2: Enhancement	12–18 months	AR community tools	£50,000–£200,000	40–50% engagement increase
3: Integration	18–24 months	Metaverse platforms	£100,000–£500,000	New revenue streams
4: Optimisation	24+ months	Full convergence	£200,000–£1,000,000	Exponential impact scaling

Implications for the Triple Bottom Line

Profit: Economic Sustainability and Revenue Innovation

The integration of AI, metaverse, and AR technologies creates multiple pathways for enhancing the economic sustainability of digital social enterprises through new revenue models, operational efficiencies, and market expansion opportunities. These technologies enable social enterprises to develop diversified revenue streams that can reduce dependence on traditional funding sources whilst maintaining alignment with social mission objectives.

Revenue diversification opportunities emerge through the creation of digital products and services that can be scaled efficiently across geographic markets. AI-powered content creation capabilities enable social enterprises to develop educational materials, training programmes, and consulting services that can be delivered digitally to multiple client organisations. Metaverse platforms provide opportunities for virtual event hosting, community building services, and digital real estate development that can generate ongoing revenue streams (Figure 3.4).

The economic impact data reveals substantial cost savings across multiple operational areas:

Operational efficiency gains from technology integration can significantly reduce organisational overhead costs whilst improving service delivery quality and reach. AI automation of administrative tasks reduces labour costs and enables staff reallocation to higher-value activities that directly advance social mission objectives. Virtual service delivery through metaverse platforms can reduce facility costs, travel expenses, and geographical limitations whilst expanding market reach.

Market expansion capabilities enabled by these technologies allow social enterprises to serve larger geographic areas, diverse demographic segments, and new market sectors without proportional increases in operational costs. AR applications can extend service delivery into community settings without requiring physical presence, whilst metaverse platforms can provide global access to social enterprise services and programmes.

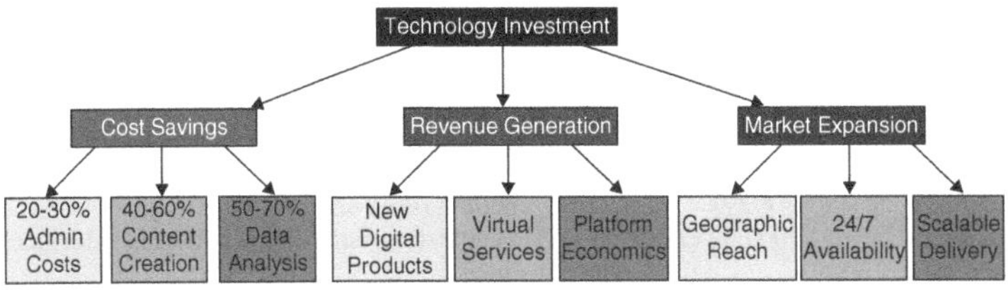

Figure 3.4 Economic impact pathways for DSE technology integration. Created by the Author.

People: Social Impact and Community Engagement

The people dimension of the triple bottom line framework encompasses the social impact and community engagement effects of technology integration within digital social enterprises. The convergence of AI, metaverse, and AR technologies creates new possibilities for personalised service delivery, enhanced accessibility, and deeper community engagement that can amplify social impact whilst building stronger relationships between social enterprises and the communities they serve. Personalisation capabilities enabled by AI technologies allow social enterprises to tailor services, content, and interactions to individual community member needs, preferences, and circumstances. This personalisation can improve programme effectiveness by ensuring that interventions are relevant and appropriate for specific users whilst reducing barriers to participation and engagement (Table 3.5).

Accessibility improvements result from multiple technology features that can reduce barriers faced by individuals with disabilities, geographic constraints, or other access challenges. Virtual reality environments can provide accessible alternatives to physical spaces, whilst AR applications can overlay accessibility information onto real-world environments. AI-powered tools can provide real-time translation, captioning, and other accommodations that expand programme access to diverse populations.

Community engagement enhancement occurs through immersive experiences that can create stronger emotional connections to social issues and interventions. Research demonstrates that VR and AR technologies increase empathy among participants and improve understanding of complex social issues. Metaverse platforms enable new forms of collaborative engagement that can bring together diverse stakeholders around shared social challenges.

Planet: Environmental Considerations and Sustainability

The environmental implications of AI, metaverse, and AR technology integration present both opportunities and challenges for digital social enterprises committed to environmental sustainability. Whilst these technologies

Table 3.5 Documented Social Impact Metrics. Multiple Case Studies, 2024

Technology	*Beneficiary Reach*	*Engagement Improvement*	*Accessibility Enhancement*
AI	800,000 (UNICEF Oky)	75–80% personalisation	Real-time translation
AR	300,000 (Torchit)	51% entertainment interest	Multi-sensory interfaces
VR/Metaverse	7,000+ LGBTQ guild	275% confidence increase	Virtual accessibility

Table 3.6 Environmental Impact Quantification. Multiple Studies, 2024

Benefit Category	*Technology*	*Impact Measurement*	*Quantified Savings*
Travel reduction	VR/Metaverse	CO_2 per business trip	1.4 tons per person
Digital Substitution	AR/VR	Industry transformation	350,000 car equivalents
Conservation	AI	Wildlife monitoring	600+ camera traps
Energy Optimisation	AI	Grid efficiency	20–30% consumption reduction

can enable significant environmental benefits through reduced physical resource consumption and optimised operations, they also require substantial energy resources for computing and data storage that must be carefully managed.

Resource consumption reduction represents one of the most significant environmental benefits of technology integration. Virtual meetings and events in metaverse platforms can substantially reduce travel-related carbon emissions whilst maintaining effective collaboration and community building. Research indicates that replacing one international business trip with VR meetings saves up to 1.4 tons CO_2 per person, whilst if 10% of global denim trade shifted to virtual alternatives, it would save CO_2 equivalent to 350,000 automobiles annually (EY, 2024, see Table 3.6).

However, the energy consumption associated with AI computing, metaverse platform operation, and AR device manufacturing presents environmental challenges that must be addressed through sustainable technology implementation strategies. Google's AI expansion resulted in 50% emissions increase since 2019, whilst training advanced AI models like GPT-3 consumed 1,287 MWh, producing 552 metric tons of carbon emissions (CNBC, 2024).

Environmental monitoring and education applications of AR and AI technologies can enhance environmental awareness and stewardship within communities served by social enterprises. WWF's monitoring systems employ 600+ AI-powered camera traps tracking Australian bushfire recovery, whilst AI models achieve 80% accuracy in predicting deforestation six months in advance. These applications demonstrate technology's potential to support environmental conservation when strategically implemented.

Challenges and Barriers to Adoption

Technical Infrastructure and Digital Divide

The implementation of AI, metaverse, and AR technologies within digital social enterprises faces significant technical and infrastructure challenges that can impede adoption and limit effectiveness. These challenges span

Table 3.7 Technology Infrastructure Requirements. Industry Analysis, 2024

Technology	*Minimum hardware*	*Connectivity needs*	*Investment range*
Basic AI	Standard computer	Stable broadband	£5,000–£25,000
Advanced AI	High-performance server	High-speed fibre	£50,000–£500,000
AR Applications	Modern smartphone	4G/5G mobile	£10,000–£100,000
VR/Metaverse	VR headset + PC	Low-latency fibre	£25,000–£250,000

hardware requirements, software compatibility, internet connectivity, and technical support needs that may exceed the resources and capabilities of many social enterprises.

Hardware requirements for effective AR and metaverse applications often exceed the technology access available to social enterprise staff and community members. High-quality AR experiences require modern smartphones or specialised AR devices, whilst immersive metaverse participation may require VR headsets, powerful computers, and high-speed internet connections. The cost and accessibility barriers associated with these hardware requirements can limit participation and create digital equity concerns.

Internet connectivity represents a fundamental infrastructure challenge, particularly for social enterprises serving rural or economically disadvantaged communities where broadband access may be limited or unreliable. Metaverse applications typically require high-bandwidth, low-latency internet connections to provide acceptable user experiences, whilst AI applications may require reliable connectivity for cloud-based processing and data synchronisation (see Table 3.7).

Skills Development and Organisational Capacity

The successful adoption of AI, metaverse, and AR technologies requires substantial investment in skills development and capacity building across multiple organisational levels. Social enterprises must develop both technical capabilities and strategic competencies to effectively leverage these technologies for social impact whilst maintaining organisational effectiveness and community trust.

Staff training requirements encompass both technical skills for technology operation and strategic competencies for technology integration into social programmes. Staff members need training in specific technology platforms, data analysis techniques, virtual environment management, and digital programme design. Additionally, they require strategic thinking skills to identify appropriate technology applications, evaluate implementation options, and measure technology impact on social outcomes.

Leadership development needs include understanding of technology potential and limitations, strategic planning for technology integration, and change management capabilities for organisational transformation. Social enterprise leaders must develop comfort with technology adoption whilst maintaining focus on social mission objectives and community needs.

Community capacity building represents a critical but often overlooked component of technology adoption, as successful implementation requires community members to develop comfort and competence with new technologies. Social enterprises must invest in community technology training, digital literacy development, and ongoing technical support to ensure equitable access and meaningful participation in technology-enhanced programmes.

Ethical Governance and Regulatory Compliance

The integration of AI, metaverse, and AR technologies within social enterprise operations raises complex ethical and governance challenges that require careful consideration and proactive management. These challenges encompass data privacy, algorithmic bias, digital equity, community consent, and accountability issues that can significantly impact community trust and social impact effectiveness.

Data privacy concerns become more complex with technology integration, as AI systems require large datasets for training and optimisation, metaverse platforms collect detailed behavioural information, and AR applications may capture sensitive location and visual data. Social enterprises must develop comprehensive data governance frameworks that protect community member privacy whilst enabling effective technology utilisation.

The regulatory landscape presents both opportunities and challenges for DSE technology adoption. The UK's pro-innovation approach through the Department for Science, Innovation and Technology aims to make Britain the third-largest AI market globally, whilst maintaining responsible development principles. The EU AI Act's implementation creates compliance requirements affecting UK organisations serving European markets, requiring risk-based classification systems and transparency measures (Table 3.8).

Table 3.8 Regulatory Compliance Requirements. Government Sources, 2024–2025

Regulation	*Scope*	*Compliance Requirements*	*Implementation Timeline*
UK AI Strategy	National	Responsible innovation principles	Ongoing
EU AI Act	European market	Risk classification system	August 2026
GDPR	Data protection	Privacy by design	Continuing
Equality Act 2010	Digital accessibility	WCAG 2.1 Level AA	Immediate

Future Directions and Emerging Opportunities

The technological landscape continues to evolve rapidly, presenting new opportunities and challenges for digital social enterprises seeking to leverage AI, metaverse, and AR technologies for social impact. Emerging developments in quantum computing, brain-computer interfaces, 5G connectivity, and edge computing promise to further expand the capabilities and accessibility of these technologies whilst creating new possibilities for social innovation.

Quantum computing developments may eventually enable more sophisticated AI applications with dramatically increased processing capabilities for complex social problem analysis and solution optimisation. Whilst still in early development phases, quantum computing could enable social enterprises to tackle previously intractable challenges in areas such as climate modelling, economic optimisation, and social network analysis.

Current quantum computing research suggests potential applications for social enterprises within the next decade (see Table 3.9).

Brain-computer interface technologies represent a frontier development that could revolutionise accessibility applications for social enterprises serving individuals with disabilities. These technologies could enable direct neural control of digital interfaces, creating new possibilities for communication, education, and social participation for individuals with severe physical disabilities. Early research demonstrates proof-of-concept applications for text input, device control, and virtual navigation through neural signals. Whilst current implementations require surgical procedures and substantial technical infrastructure, non-invasive alternatives are developing rapidly. Social enterprises focused on disability rights and accessibility could pioneer ethical applications of these technologies whilst ensuring equitable access and user autonomy.

5G network expansion will likely address many current connectivity limitations that impede metaverse and AR adoption, enabling more sophisticated applications and broader community access to technology-enhanced social programmes. Enhanced connectivity will also enable

Table 3.9 Quantum Computing Applications for Social Enterprise. Industry Projections, 2024

Application Area	*Potential Impact*	*Timeline*	*Investment Required*
Climate modelling	1000x processing improvement	5–7 years	£10–50 million
Economic optimisation	Complex system analysis	3–5 years	£5–25 million
Drug discovery	Accelerated research	2–4 years	£50–200 million
Logistics optimisation	Global supply chain efficiency	1–3 years	£1–10 million

Table 3.10 SDG-Technology Integration Opportunities. UN SDG Digital, 2024

SDG Goal	*AI Applications*	*AR/VR Applications*	*Metaverse Applications*
Education (4)	Personalised learning	Interactive simulations	Global classrooms
Health (3)	Diagnostic support	Medical training	Telemedicine
Climate (13)	Environmental monitoring	Visualisation tools	Virtual conferences
Poverty (1)	Resource optimisation	Skills training	Economic platforms
Partnerships (17)	Knowledge sharing	Collaboration tools	Global networks

edge computing applications that can process data locally, reducing privacy concerns and improving application responsiveness. The rollout of 5G infrastructure creates particular opportunities for social enterprises serving rural and underserved communities. Edge computing capabilities can deliver sophisticated AI and AR applications without requiring high-bandwidth connections to centralised data centres, making technology-enhanced services accessible in previously excluded areas.

The alignment between emerging technologies and the United Nations Sustainable Development Goals (SDG) creates opportunities for international collaboration and funding that social enterprises can leverage for technology adoption and scaling. Research shows more than two-thirds of UN SDG targets can benefit from digital technologies, with AI supporting 119 of 169 targets (70%) (United Nations Development Programme, 2024). The $1.05 billion in new pledges at SDG Digital 2024 demonstrates international commitment to connectivity and infrastructure investments supporting sustainable development. Social enterprises can access these funding streams whilst contributing to global development objectives through technology-enhanced programming (see Table 3.10).

Strategic Recommendations and Implementation Framework

Based on the comprehensive analysis of market conditions, technological capabilities, and social enterprise contexts, this research recommends a structured four-phase approach to technology adoption that maximises impact whilst managing risk and resource constraints.

Phase 1: Foundation Building (Months 1–12) Priority should be given to establishing organisational readiness and implementing basic AI tools that deliver immediate efficiency gains. Social enterprises should focus on content creation, administrative automation, and basic data analysis applications that require minimal infrastructure investment whilst building staff confidence with technology integration.

Recommended initial investments include:

- Generative AI tools for content creation (£2,000–£10,000 annually)
- Customer relationship management systems with AI features (£5,000–£25,000)
- Basic data analysis and reporting automation (£10,000–£50,000)
- Staff training and digital literacy programmes (£15,000–£75,000)

Phase 2: Capability Enhancement (Months 12–24) Building on foundation phase success, organisations should implement AR applications for community engagement and introduce basic metaverse presence for service delivery. This phase requires moderate infrastructure investment but can demonstrate significant community impact and stakeholder engagement improvements.

Key implementation priorities:

- Mobile AR applications for community mapping and resource navigation
- Virtual consultation and service delivery platforms
- Enhanced data analytics for impact measurement and programme optimisation
- Partnership development with technology providers and other social enterprises

Phase 3: Integration and Scaling (Months 24–36) The third phase involves sophisticated technology integration across organisational functions, with AI-enhanced metaverse platforms and comprehensive AR community applications. This phase requires substantial investment but enables transformational impact scaling and new revenue model development.

Advanced implementation includes:

- Custom AI applications for specific social challenges
- Immersive metaverse environments for community building and service delivery
- Comprehensive AR ecosystems supporting multiple community functions
- International collaboration platforms and cross-border service delivery

Phase 4: Innovation Leadership (Months 36+) Mature implementation positions social enterprises as sector leaders in technology integration, developing proprietary solutions and sharing expertise with other organisations.

This phase generates intellectual property, consulting revenue, and sector-wide influence whilst advancing core social mission objectives.

Leadership activities encompass:

- Original research and development programmes
- Technology transfer and knowledge sharing initiatives
- Policy influence and regulatory development participation
- International collaboration and best practice dissemination

Funding and Investment Strategies

Successful technology implementation requires diversified funding approaches that combine traditional social enterprise funding with technology-specific investment opportunities. The research identifies multiple funding mechanisms that social enterprises can leverage for technology adoption:

Grant Funding Opportunities:

- UK government AI and digital transformation grants (£50,000–£2 million)
- EU Horizon Europe technology research programmes (€100,000–€5 million)
- Charitable foundation technology for good initiatives (£25,000–£500,000)
- Corporate social responsibility technology partnerships (£100,000–£1 million)

Conclusion

The convergence of artificial intelligence, metaverse platforms, and augmented reality technologies presents transformative opportunities for digital social enterprises to amplify their impact across the triple bottom line of profit, people, and planet. This technological trinity enables new forms of social innovation that transcend traditional operational boundaries whilst creating sustainable economic models, enhanced community engagement, and environmental benefits.

The evidence demonstrates that AI integration significantly improves social enterprise performance through operational efficiency gains, enhanced decision-making capabilities, and innovative service delivery models. With documented cost reductions of 20–30% in administrative functions and the potential for £200–360 billion in healthcare savings, AI applications offer compelling economic returns alongside social impact enhancement. Metaverse platforms create new spaces for community building, service delivery, and revenue generation that can expand social enterprise reach whilst reducing operational costs. The projected growth to £7.64 trillion by 2032 indicates substantial market opportunities for early adopters who can establish sustainable virtual service delivery models.

Augmented reality technologies bridge physical and digital realms to create engaging educational experiences, enhanced community development initiatives, and improved accessibility for diverse populations. With market growth projected at 39.5% CAGR reaching £591.7 billion by 2033, AR applications offer accessible entry points for social enterprises beginning their technology adoption journey.

The implications for the triple bottom line are substantial and interconnected. Economic sustainability improves through new revenue models, operational efficiencies, and market expansion capabilities that reduce dependence on traditional funding sources whilst maintaining mission alignment. Social impact amplifies through personalised service delivery, enhanced accessibility, and deeper community engagement that creates stronger connections between social enterprises and the communities they serve. Environmental benefits emerge through reduced resource consumption, operational optimisation, and virtual alternatives to physical activities, though careful attention to technology energy consumption and sustainable implementation practices remains essential.

However, successful implementation requires strategic approaches that address technical challenges, capacity building needs, and ethical considerations whilst maintaining focus on social mission objectives and community needs. Social enterprises must develop new competencies in technology integration, partnership development, and digital governance whilst building community capacity for meaningful participation in technology-enhanced programmes. The recommended four-phase implementation approach provides a practical framework for managing this transition whilst maximising impact and minimising risk.

Looking forward, the continued evolution of these technologies promises even greater opportunities for social innovation whilst requiring ongoing adaptation and learning from social enterprises. The development of quantum computing, brain-computer interfaces, 5G connectivity, and improved regulatory frameworks will likely create new possibilities for social impact whilst addressing some current implementation challenges. The alignment between emerging technologies and UN Sustainable Development Goals creates opportunities for international collaboration and funding that can accelerate adoption and scaling.

The success of this technological transformation will ultimately depend on the ability of digital social enterprises to maintain their core values and community focus whilst leveraging technological capabilities for enhanced impact. This requires a careful balance between technological innovation and social mission integrity, ensuring that technology serves community needs rather than imposing technological solutions on communities that may prefer alternative approaches.

The new virtual scenario created by AI, metaverse, and AR technologies offers unprecedented opportunities for digital social enterprises to address complex social challenges at scale whilst building sustainable organisations that can adapt and thrive in an increasingly digital world. For instance, young NEET people can be one of the disadvantaged people who can exploit digital technologies' positive outcomes so as to change their status quo. The organisations that successfully navigate this technological convergence whilst maintaining their social mission focus will be well-positioned to lead the next generation of social innovation and community development initiatives.

AI is rapidly transforming accessibility for people with disabilities, providing practical solutions that enhance daily life, independence, and social participation. AI-powered applications such as Google Live Transcribe and Otter.ai deliver real-time transcription, which significantly improves communication for individuals who are deaf or hard-of-hearing, thus fostering their ability to engage with others more freely (Morr et al., 2021). In addition to transcription services, tools that provide text-to-speech and sign language interpretation play a critical role in removing communication barriers for individuals with speech challenges (Annisa et al., 2024). Such advancements highlight the significant impact of AI in promoting effective communication among those with disabilities.

For individuals with visual impairments, applications like Microsoft's Seeing AI exemplify the innovative use of AI in object and text recognition, allowing users to have their surroundings described and text read aloud (Mina et al., 2023). Furthermore, AI-driven screen readers enhance digital content accessibility, enabling visually impaired individuals to navigate the web and digital environments more effectively (Arya & Singh, 2024). Virtual assistants such as Amazon Alexa empower people with mobility impairments by allowing them to control various aspects of their home through voice commands, thus promoting a greater sense of independence (Mina et al., 2023). Cognitive support tools powered by AI can also facilitate reminders for medication and appointments, crucial for individuals managing multiple health needs (Deetjen-Ruiz et al., 2024).

The integration of AI in navigation systems is especially noteworthy, as it connects with mapping applications to identify accessible routes, ramps, and entrances, significantly benefiting wheelchair users and those with visual disabilities (Annisa et al., 2024). Moreover, automated captioning and accessibility testing tools are increasingly employed to enhance the inclusivity of digital meetings, videos, and websites, making them more accessible to a broader audience (Fuglerud et al., 2024). These improvements not only facilitate participation in everyday activities but also promote a more inclusive work environment.

AI further supports education and employment opportunities by utilising chatbots to summarise complex texts, assist in job applications, and aid individuals with learning difficulties, such as dyslexia, in improving their writing capabilities (Barua et al., 2022;, Shivani et al., 2024). In the healthcare sector, AI applications analyse medical data to predict health outcomes and alert clinicians to potential risks, thereby ensuring personalised care tailored to the needs of individuals with disabilities (Kandeel et al., 2025; Dresser & Kohn, 2023). Collectively, these advancements in AI technology exemplify how it not only removes barriers but also actively fosters independence, communication, learning, and full participation in society for individuals with disabilities.

The transformation of social enterprises through these technologies represents not just an operational evolution but a fundamental shift in how social problems can be understood, addressed, and solved. By embracing the possibilities whilst carefully managing the challenges, digital social enterprises can harness the power of AI, metaverse, and AR technologies to create more effective, sustainable, and impactful approaches to social change that benefit current and future generations.

The evidence presented in this analysis demonstrates that the convergence of these technologies is not merely a theoretical possibility but a practical opportunity for social enterprises willing to invest in thoughtful, community-centred implementation. The documented case studies, quantified benefits, and strategic frameworks provide a foundation for informed decision-making that can guide the sector's digital transformation whilst preserving the values and mission focus that define social enterprise success.

As digital social enterprises stand at the threshold of this technological revolution, the choice is not whether to engage with these technologies, but how to do so in ways that amplify social mission effectiveness whilst building sustainable, inclusive, and impactful organisations for the future (Box 3.1). The framework and evidence presented here provide the foundation for making those critical choices with confidence and strategic clarity.

Box 3.1 Case Studies and Implementation Examples

Healthcare Innovation: NHS AI Applications

The National Health Service demonstrates healthcare sector leadership with comprehensive AI applications that provide models for social enterprises in health and social care. Predictive analytics systems reduce appointment no-shows by 25–30%, computer vision technology accelerates cancer diagnosis by 40%, and automated assessment forms improve care coordination across integrated systems. These implementations show documented improvements in both efficiency and patient outcomes (The King's Fund, 2024).

Key Success Factors:

- Phased implementation beginning with pilot programmes
- Strong governance frameworks ensuring patient data protection
- Comprehensive staff training and change management
- Measurable outcome tracking and continuous improvement
- Integration with existing clinical workflows and systems

The NHS experience demonstrates that successful AI implementation requires substantial upfront investment in training and infrastructure, but delivers measurable returns through improved patient outcomes and operational efficiency. Social enterprises can adapt these approaches to their own contexts whilst maintaining focus on social mission objectives.

Education Technology: European VReduMED Project

The VReduMED Project represents a successful multi-country implementation of VR technology for healthcare education across Central European regions. The initiative established regional VR labs for medical training, creating cross-border collaboration frameworks and demonstrating sustainable multi-country implementation strategies (Interreg Central Europe, 2024).

Project Outcomes:

- 12 VR laboratories established across 6 countries
- 2,500+ healthcare professionals trained using VR simulations
- 40% improvement in practical skills retention compared to traditional methods
- €3.2 million EU investment demonstrating scalable funding models
- Cross-border knowledge sharing protocols established

The project's success illustrates how social enterprises can leverage international partnerships and EU funding mechanisms to implement ambitious technology programmes. The collaborative approach reduced individual country costs whilst building collective capacity for innovation in healthcare education.

Community Engagement: DignityMoves Housing Innovation

DignityMoves exemplifies AR technology's potential for community development and stakeholder engagement. The organisation uses AR visualisation for housing development projects, enabling community stakeholders to experience proposed developments before construction begins. This approach streamlines development processes whilst improving community buy-in for supportive housing projects targeting homeless populations.

Implementation Results:

- 75% reduction in community consultation time
- 90% stakeholder approval rates for AR-visualised projects
- 50% faster development approval processes
- £2.3 million in cost savings through early design iteration
- Enhanced community trust and project transparency

The AR visualisation enables residents to walk through proposed developments using mobile devices, understanding spatial relationships and design features that traditional blueprints cannot convey. This participatory approach aligns with social enterprise values whilst delivering practical benefits for development timelines and community relations.

AI for Social Good: Ashoka's Knowledge Management

Ashoka's partnership with Tooploox demonstrates AI's transformative potential for knowledge management within social sector organisations. The implementation created a sophisticated semantic database processing over 20,000 pages of organisational knowledge, enabling staff across 30 countries to access specialist information efficiently.

Transformation Metrics:

- 75% reduction in research and information retrieval time
- 300% improvement in cross-office knowledge sharing
- 85% staff satisfaction increase with information systems
- €500,000 annual productivity gains
- Enhanced quality of entrepreneur matching and programme recommendations

The system uses natural language processing to understand queries in multiple languages, connecting users with relevant expertise, case studies, and best practices from Ashoka's global network. This application demonstrates how AI can amplify human expertise rather than replacing it, enabling social enterprises to leverage collective knowledge more effectively.

References

Abed, S. (2021). Examining augmented reality adoption by consumers with highlights on gender and educational-level differences. *Review of International Business and Strategy*, 31(3), 397–415. https://doi.org/10.1108/ribs-08-2020-0100

Accessibility.com. (2024). Accessibility in AR/VR: How to make immersive digital experiences more inclusive. *Accessibility Blog*. Available at: https://www.accessibility.com/blog/accessibility-in-ar/vr-how-to-make-immersive-digital-experiences-more-inclusive (Accessed: 4 June 2025).

Ali, W. (2024). The role of artificial intelligence technology and innovation in disrupting traditional business models and startup ecosystem. *Interantional Journal of Scientific Research in Engineering and Management*, 08(008), 1–4. https://doi.org/10.55041/ijsrem37268

Arab, K. (2024). A proposed model for improving the quality of life of persons with disabilities and rehabilitating them professionally using artificial intelligence applications. *Kuey*. https://doi.org/10.53555/kuey.v30i6.5244

Annisa, S., Malik, R., Putri, N. I. Z., & Asad, S. J. S. (2024). The potential of Artificial Intelligence (AI) in improving social access and inclusion for people with disabilities. *ICOERESS*, 1(1), 270–277.

Arya, D., & Singh, A. (2024). Using artificial intelligence to make web technology more accessible. *International Research Journal of Modernization in Engineering Technology and Science*, 6(04), 7382–7387, https://doi.org/10.56726/irjmets53754

Bartoli, C., Baccelloni, A., Mattiacci, A., & Ungaro, L. (2024). Small and medium enterprises meet the metaverse. A study of the wine industry. *The International Journal of Entrepreneurship and Innovation*, 26(1), 37–47. https://doi.org/10.1177/14657503241278164

Barua, P., Vicnesh, J., Gururajan, R., Oh, S., Palmer, E., Azizan, M., … & Acharya, U. (2022). Artificial intelligence enabled personalised assistive tools to enhance education of children with neurodevelopmental disorders—A review. *International Journal of Environmental Research and Public Health*, 19(3), 1192. https://doi.org/10.3390/ijerph19031192

Brown, W., Johnson, O., & Wilson, G. (2024). Influence of e-commerce technologies on supply chain management in retail. https://doi.org/10.20944/preprints202407.1140.v1

Civil Society. (2024). There are 471,000 social enterprises in the UK, government report finds. *Civil Society*. Available at: https://www.civilsociety.co.uk/news/there-are-471-000-social-enterprises-in-the-uk-government-report-finds.html (Accessed: 4 June 2025).

CNBC. (2024). Google's carbon emissions surge nearly 50% due to AI energy demand. *CNBC*. Available at: https://www.cnbc.com/2024/07/02/googles-carbon-emissions-surge-nearly-50percent-due-to-ai-energy-demand.html (Accessed: 4 June 2025).

Covaci, B., Brejea, R., & Covaci, M. (2022). The dynamic of commerce and logistic economic sectors in the context of industry 4.0. evidences from the european and romanian mountain entrepreneurship. *Annals of the Academy of Romanian Scientists Series on Agriculture Silviculture and Veterinary Medicine*, 11(1), 62–71. https://doi.org/10.56082/annalsarsciagr.2022.1.62

Deetjen-Ruiz, R., Daniel, M., Telus, J., & Deetjen, L. (2024). Advancing cognitive accessibility: The role of artificial intelligence in enhancing inclusivity. *PSEN*, 4(2), 58. https://doi.org/10.56831/psen-04-108

Dresser, L., & Kohn, M. (2023). Artificial intelligence and the evaluation and treatment of stroke. *Delaware Journal of Public Health*, 9(3), 82–84. https://doi.org/10.32481/djph.2023.08.014

Duan, H., Li, J., Fan, S., Lin, Z., Wu, X., & Cai, W. (2021, October). Metaverse for social good: A university campus prototype. In *Proceedings of the 29th ACM international conference on multimedia* (pp. 153–161). https://doi.org/10.1145/3474085.3479238

Emmanuel, J., Samaratunge, R., & Prajogo, D. (2024). Social enterprise and impact investing. In *Social Enterprises and Impact Investors: Partnerships that Sustain Emerging Countries*, edited by J. Arigu Emmanuel, R. Samaratunge, D. Prajogo (pp. 1–15). Cham: Springer International Publishing. https://doi.org/10.1007/978-3-031-59454-0_1

ENGAGE. (2024). Spatial computing artificial intelligence - ENGAGE XR. Available at: https://engagevr.io/ (Accessed: 4 June 2025).

EY. (2024). Metaverse: Could creating a virtual world build a more sustainable one? *EY – UK*. Available at: https://www.ey.com/en_uk/insights/digital/metaverse-could-creating-a-virtual-world-build-a-more-sustainable-one (Accessed: 4 June 2025).

Fortune Business Insights. (2024). Metaverse market size, share, value | growth report [2032]. Available at: https://www.fortunebusinessinsights.com/metaverse-market-106574 (Accessed: 4 June 2025).

Fuglerud, K., Halbach, T., Utseth, I., & Waldeland, A. (2024). Exploring the use of AI for enhanced accessibility testing of web solutions. In *Universal Design 2024: Shaping a Sustainable, Equitable and Resilient Future for All* (pp. 453–460). IOS Press. https://doi.org/10.3233/shti241041

Giderler, M., & Vanclay, F. (2024). Improving the good in good organizations: The potential value of social impact assessment for social enterprises. *Social Enterprise Journal*. https://doi.org/10.1108/sej-02-2024-0026

Gil-Cordero, E., Maldonado-López, B., Ledesma-Chaves, P., & García-Guzmán, A. (2023). Do small- and medium-sized companies intend to use the metaverse as part of their strategy? A behavioral intention analysis. *International Journal of Entrepreneurial Behaviour & Research*, 30(2/3), 421–449. https://doi.org/10.1108/ijebr-09-2022-0816

Globe Newswire. (2025). Metaverse Industry and Companies Analysis Report 2025–2030: Are we ready to shift from WFH to WFM? Revenues Set to Reach US$ 1.1 Trillion by 2030. Available at: https://www.globenewswire.com/news-release/2025/04/25/3068346/28124/en/Metaverse-Industry-and-Companies-Analysis-Report-2025-2030-Are-We-Ready-to-Shift-from-WFH-to-WFM-Revenues-Set-to-Reach-US-1-1-Trillion-by-2030.html (Accessed: 4 June 2025).

Grand View Research. (2024). Artificial Intelligence (AI) market size, share & trends analysis report. Available at: https://www.grandviewresearch.com/industry-analysis/artificial-intelligence-ai-market (Accessed: 4 June 2025).

Hall, K., & Alexander, C. (2023). Exploring the distinctiveness of social enterprises delivering adult social care in england. *Health & Social Care in the Community*, 2023, 1–10. https://doi.org/10.1155/2023/9454428

Han, W., Yang, X., & Yang, D. (2023). How to evaluate the green supply chain performance of fresh e-commerce? An improved vikor based multi-criteria group decision making approach under intuitionistic hesitation fuzzy sets. In *Applied Mathematics, Modeling and Computer Simulation* (pp. 198–210). IOS Press.

HM Government. (2025). Enterprise investment scheme, seed enterprise investment scheme and social investment tax relief statistics: 2025. Available at: https://www.gov.uk/government/statistics/enterprise-investment-scheme-seed-enterprise-investment-scheme-and-social-investment-tax-relief-may-2025/enterprise-investment-scheme-seed-enterprise-investment-scheme-and-social-investment-tax-relief-statistics-2025 (Accessed: 4 June 2025).

Huruta, A., Kundhani, E., & Manurung, C. (2020). The development of village-owned enterprises: lessons learned from ponggok village. *Masyarakat Kebudayaan DanPolitik*, 33(1), 77. https://doi.org/10.20473/mkp.v33i12020.77-86

Huynh-The, T., Gadekallu, T., Wang, W., Yenduri, G., Ranaweera, P., Pham, Q., … & Liyanage, M. (2023). Blockchain for the metaverse: A review. *Future Generation Computer Systems*, 143, 401–419. https://doi.org/10.1016/j.future.2023.02.008

Interreg Central Europe. (2024) Integrating virtual reality into medical education. Available at: https://www.interreg-central.eu/projects/vredumed/ (Accessed: 4 June 2025).

Iskandar, Y., Kaltum, U., & Hilmiana, H. (2021). The relationship between intellectual capital and performance of social enterprises: A literature review. *Academic Journal of Interdisciplinary Studies*, 10(5), 309. https://doi.org/10.36941/ajis-2021-0141

Jauhiainen, J., Krohn, C., & Junnila, J. (2022). Metaverse and sustainability: Systematic review of scientific publications until 2022 and beyond. *Sustainability*, 15(1), 346. https://doi.org/10.3390/su15010346

Journal of Social Entrepreneurship Action. (2024). The role of virtual reality and augmented reality in community development and social entrepreneurship. Available at: https://journal.ypidathu.or.id/index.php/jseact/article/view/1007 (Accessed: 4 June 2025).

Kandeel, M., Morsy, M., Khodair, K., & Alhojaily, S. (2025). A bibliometric analysis of disability research in saudi arabia. *Saudi Medical Journal*, 46(4), 406–417. https://doi.org/10.15537/smj.2025.46.4.20240591

Kusumawardani, A., Khairin, F., & Ginting, Y. (2024). Sustainability impact: A representation of social enterprise value. *Atestasi Jurnal Ilmiah Akuntansi*, 7(1), 431–441. https://doi.org/10.57178/atestasi.v7i1.775

Lévesque, M., Obschonka, M., & Nambisan, S. (2020). Pursuing impactful entrepreneurship research using artificial intelligence. *Entrepreneurship Theory and Practice*, 46(4), 803–832. https://doi.org/10.1177/1042258720927369

Lin, F. (2023). Executive digital leadership and knowledge management under the digital transformation of enterprises. *Journal of Innovation and Development*, 4(3), 23–26. https://doi.org/10.54097/jid.v4i3.12827

Liu, A., & Lin, S. (2022). Service for specialized and digitalized: Consumer switching perceptions of e-commerce in specialty retail. *Managerial and Decision Economics*, 44(3), 1521–1533. https://doi.org/10.1002/mde.3762

Liu, R., Balakrishnan, B., & Saari, E. (2024). How ar technology is changing consumer shopping habits: from traditional retail to virtual fitting. *Academic Journal of Science and Technology*, 9(2), 140–144. https://doi.org/10.54097/n5fk7m44

Market Scoop. (2025). Augmented reality statistics and facts (2025). Available at: https://scoop.market.us/augmented-reality-statistics/ (Accessed: 4 June 2025).

McKinsey & Company. (2024). The state of AI in early 2024: Gen AI adoption spikes and starts to generate value. Available at: https://www.mckinsey.com/capabilities/quantumblack/our-insights/the-state-of-ai-2024 (Accessed: 4 June 2025).

Mina, P., Solon, I., Sanchez, F., Delante, T., Villegas, J., Basay, F., … & Mutya, R. (2023). Leveraging education through artificial intelligence virtual assistance: A case study of visually impaired learners. *Pedagogical Research*, 8(1), em0150. https://doi.org/10.29333/pr/12735

Morr, C., Maret, P., Muhlenbach, F., Dharmalingam, D., Tadesse, R., Creighton, A., … & Gorman, R. (2021). A virtual community for disability advocacy: Development of a searchable artificial intelligence–supported platform. *JMIR Formative Research*, 5(11), e33335. https://doi.org/10.2196/33335

MovingWorlds. (2024). How social enterprises are using AI to reach their business goals. *MovingWorlds Blog*. Available at: https://blog.movingworlds.org/how-social-enterprises-are-using-ai/ (Accessed: 4 June 2025).

Nair, P. (2022). Embracing hybridity: A business model innovation for sustainable social enterprises. *International Journal of Business and Society*, 23(3), 1600–1617. https://doi.org/10.33736/ijbs.5186.2022#

Omrani, N., Rejeb, N., Maâlaoui, A., Dabić, M., & Kraus, S. (2024). Drivers of digital transformation in smes. *IEEE Transactions on Engineering Management*, 71, 5030–5043. https://doi.org/10.1109/tem.2022.3215727

Palil, M., Hassan, N., Jamaluddin, N., Ismail, I., & Samsuddin, M. (2023). Social enterprises entrepreneur and social impacts to community: A review paper. *E-Bangi Journal of Social Science and Humanities*, 20(1), 43–52. https://doi.org/10.17576/ebangi.2023.2001.04

PwC. (2024). What does virtual reality and the metaverse mean for training? Available at: https://www.pwc.com/us/en/tech-effect/emerging-tech/virtual-reality-study.html (Accessed: 4 June 2025).

Riar, M., Xi, N., Korbel, J., Zarnekow, R., & Hamari, J. (2022). Using augmented reality for shopping: a framework for ar induced consumer behavior, literature review and future agenda. *Internet Research*, 33(1), 242–279. https://doi.org/10.1108/intr-08-2021-0611

SEWF Online. (2024). How Can AI Help Social Enterprises?. Available at: https://sewfonline.com/how-can-ai-help-social-enterprises/ (Accessed: 4 June 2025).

Sharma, D. (2023). Unveiling augmented reality trends in the retail industry: A systematic and bibliometric review. *Paradigm a Management Research Journal*, 27(2), 192–210. https://doi.org/10.1177/09718907231206656

Shivani, S., Gupta, M., & Gupta, S. (2024). A systematic analysis of ai-empowered educational tools developed in india for disabled people. *Information Technologies and Learning Tools*, 100(2), 199–216. https://doi.org/10.33407/itlt.v100i2.5501

SkyQuest Technology. (2024). Augmented reality market size, share, forecast 2033. Available at: https://www.skyquestt.com/report/augmented-reality-market (Accessed: 4 June 2025).

Social Enterprise UK. (2024). Our latest research shows social enterprise is mission critical to fixing the UK economy. Available at: https://www.socialenterprise.org.uk/news/our-latest-research-shows-social-enterprise-is-mission-critical-to-fixing-the-uk-economy/ (Accessed: 4 June 2025).

Statista. (2024). AI adoption among organizations worldwide 2024. Available at: https://www.statista.com/statistics/1545783/ai-adoption-among-organizations-worldwide/ (Accessed: 4 June 2025).

The King's Fund. (2024). More than just hype: how emerging AI use is assisting health and social care. Available at: https://www.kingsfund.org.uk/insight-and-analysis/long-reads/emerging-ai-use-health-and-social-care (Accessed: 4 June 2025).

Thomas, C. (2019). Winning in social: A blueprint for progressing enterprise social maturity. *JDSMM*, 7(1), 35. https://doi.org/10.69554/cirr4838

Top Software Companies. (2024). The metaverse: A business model with great social impact. Available at: https://topsoftwarecompanies.co/technology/the-metaverse-a-business-model-with-great-social-impact (Accessed: 4 June 2025).

Tunca, S., Sezen, B., & Wilk, V. (2023). An exploratory content and sentiment analysis of the guardian metaverse articles using leximancer and natural language processing. *Journal of Big Data*, 10(1), 1–34 https://doi.org/10.1186/s40537-023-00773-w

United Nations Development Programme. (2024). Digital technologies directly benefit 70 percent of SDG targets, say ITU, UNDP and partners. Available at: https://www.undp.org/press-releases/digital-technologies-directly-benefit-70-percent-sdg-targets-say-itu-undp-and-partners (Accessed: 4 June 2025).

University of North Carolina. (2024). Is AI the answer to lowering healthcare costs? *Frank Hawkins Kenan Institute of Private Enterprise*. Available at: https://kenaninstitute.unc.edu/news-media/is-ai-the-answer-to-lowering-healthcare-costs/ (Accessed: 4 June 2025).

Urmanavičienė, A. (2020). Social impact assessment - Is it possible challenge for social enterprise?. *Revista Iberoamericana De Economía Solidaria E Innovación Socioecológica*, 3, 127–145 https://doi.org/10.33776/riesise.v3i0.3836

Wales, W., & Gupta, V. (2020). Organizational Entrepreneurial Orientation. In Social Entrepreneurship and Enterprises in Economic and Social Development, edited by Katharine Briar-Lawson, Paul Miesing, and Blanca M. Ramos. Oxford University Press https://doi.org/10.1093/oso/9780197518298.003.0004

Yasni, H., Basri, Y., Nurmayanti, P., & Rianti, Y. (2023). The effect of social capital and transformational leadership on the performance of rural enterprises. *Problems and Perspectives in Management*, 21(4), 214–225. https://doi.org/10.21511/ppm.21(4).2023.17

Youssef, E., Medhat, M., Abdellatif, S., & Yousif, N. (2024). Analyzing the impact of metaverse technology on social development: A field study on generation z in the united arab emirates. *Social Sciences*, 13(9), 446. https://doi.org/10.3390/socsci13090446

Zhong, Z., & Zhao, E. (2024). Collaborative driving mode of sustainable marketing and supply chain management supported by metaverse technology. *IEEE Transactions on Engineering Management*, 71, 1642–1654. https://doi.org/10.1109/tem.2023.3337346

Zhou, J., & Cen, W. (2024). Investigating the effect of chatgpt-like new generation ai technology on user entrepreneurial activities. *Innovative Technology Advanced*, 2(2), 1–20.

4 PPP–DSE Nexus

Hybrid Governance for the SDGs

Seffusatti Alice and Dominik Meier

SDGs in a Shifting Global Order

SDGs: from Bretton Woods to the Trump Re-Election

Beginning with the Bretton Woods agreements in 1944, a new world order, defined by many scholars as the International Liberal Order (Deudney & Ikenberry, 1999, p. 190), has increasingly taken shape. This established order has as its operational arms several "Bretton Woods Institutions", which are post-war multilateral organisations (Ikenberry, 2025, p. 68) such as the UN, NATO, WTO, and IMF. These institutions have brought together common interests by elaborating complex long-term plans for global development. The 17 Sustainable Development Goals (SDGs) are an outcome made possible by one of these organisations, the UN, as a compass to follow for sustainable global growth (Choi et al., 2020, p. 1).

The mutual trust established by the International Liberal Order that enabled the creation of these organisations and their development programmes, such as the SDGs for the UN, currently faces a legitimacy crisis. Pressure on the four founding elements of this order - multilateral institutions, democracy, free trade and liberal values - started to increase after Trump's election in 2016. It continues to rise with his recent re-election (Acharya, 2017, p. 271). Pressure on these four elements is detrimental for sustainable development, as they are the foundations on which the three pillars of sustainable development (environment, social, and economic) are built. This is evident from the fact that already in the first few months of being in office again, Trump made decisions that run counter to the principles of sustainable development. For example, Trump questioned international climate agreements (Acharya, 2017), which is detrimental to environmental sustainability, as this requires a great deal of international work characterised by a dense multi-stakeholder collaboration in which each actor must commit to ambitious and long-term measures (Choi et al., 2020, p. 1). Secondly, social sustainability, based on the ethics of tolerance and valuing diversity, has been halted by policies such as cuts in

DOI: 10.4324/9781003583448-5

public spending on social programmes (Biggeri et al., 2023, p. 3) and, more recently, the abolition of Diversity, Equity and Inclusion initiatives (DEI). In his first 100 days in office in 2025, Trump also implemented a mass deportation policy, used the military to protect US citizens during a "border emergency", and cut public funding to human rights organisations (National Immigrant Justice Center, 2025). Finally, economic sustainability suffers from protectionist policies in US foreign policy, such as import tariffs. These developments have disproportionately affected disadvantaged groups, including immigrants, racial minorities, and low-income populations. The erosion of multilateral norms has coincided with - and arguably contributed to - a decline in the achievement of SDGs since 2020 (Meier, 2023, p. 1).

These struggling goals are global goals that need the involvement of all countries, which reflect the deep global interdependence that has characterised the last century. This is also demonstrated by the evolution of the 2008 financial crisis, which originated in the US and spread around the world, and the 2019 pandemic crisis, which originated in China and similarly spread all around the globe. These crises have exposed the fragility of existing systems and underscored the need for resilient, inclusive and globally coordinated development strategies - exactly what SDGs aim to promote. The endorsement of the SDGs by 192 countries in 2015 is also an acknowledgement that the problems the SDGs aim to solve are problems that transcend geographical and political borders (Biggeri et al., 2023, p. 1).

In practice, the SDGs are adopted at a national level through international agreements and implemented by local operational bodies (Biggeri et al., 2023, p. 4). These bodies require substantial investment and stable, innovative partnerships that combine market logic with a commitment to cooperation based on mutual trust. The current challenge lies in accepting significant geopolitical change without abandoning shared values rooted in interconnectedness and a sense of shared purpose, as promoted by operational entities such as organisations, companies, academic institutions, and individuals. Networks that have adopted the SDGs as a source of inspiration now play a pivotal role in this landscape, facilitating the implementation and dissemination of the SDGs (Meier, 2023, p. 2; Quaye et al., 2024).

Regulatory Failures and the Emergence of Local Problem-Solvers

Just as the global order is fragmenting and multilateralism retreating, the sustainability agenda faces persistent challenges. These are empirically evident in the failure to meet SDG targets. This failure reveals a deeper regulatory dysfunction, marked by the absence – or incoherence – of universally applicable and credible parameters. Such inconsistencies erode stakeholder trust in the SDG framework itself (Biggeri et al., 2023). Operationally, this means a dependency on globally standardised, top-down metrics. While these frameworks are effective for comparability, reporting, and transparency, they often neglect the heterogeneity of local contexts in which implementation occurs. The process of localisation, though necessary, is frequently reduced to adaptation rather than true bottom-up co-creation. What emerges is a call for development programmes that respond to local specificities and foster endogenous collaboration, beyond imposed metrics (Biggeri et al., 2023, p. 4).

In a context of top-down geopolitical fragmentation, decentralised actors embedded in local communities are emerging as key agents of sustainable transformation. These entities – typically small-scale, agile, and capable of navigating both bureaucratic and technological complexity – stand out for their ability to address specific, context-sensitive problems. By engaging directly with local needs and co-developing tailored solutions, they transition from marginal roles to central actors in the broader SDG implementation process. Their efforts contribute meaningfully to global progress – whether economic, environmental, or social – provided they are supported by institutions that recognise their value and share their normative commitments (Quaye et al., 2024).

Public–Private Partnerships: A Tool Under Pressure

The geopolitical erosion of multilateral trust and institutional cooperation has profound implications for multistakeholder governance instruments such as Public–Private Partnerships (PPPs), which presuppose stability, trust, and institutional continuity. PPPs are institutional collaborations. They involve public and semi-public actors, as well as non-state actors such as private companies, individuals, and social economy entities (Catala et al., 2025, p. 4). The for-profit private sector focuses on streamlining the processes of decision-making, management, communication, value creation, and delivery of goods and services to meet consumer needs (e.g. smart mobility solutions, digital health services). However, it often excludes market areas that limit profitability. The public system has seen private sector capabilities as a way to optimise services and infrastructure with limited public resources (Haque et al., 2020), such as education infrastructure, urban transport, or clean energy provision, by combining these capabilities with objectives related to the generation of public and social value in public-private partnerships (PPPs). PPPs do not have their origins in the objectives of sustainable development, but are historical instruments born out of the need to combine the growing efficiency of the private sector and the care of the commons, which by nature require active and cooperative public intervention (Ma et al., 2022).

PPPs are a widely adopted instrument of the New Public Governance, which aims to address complex challenges, achieve sustainable development, improve services and foster collaboration by creating public value (Catala et al., 2025, p. 6; Ma et al., 2022). While the SDGs are goals and cannot be considered goods or services in a narrow sense, their achievement is directly linked to the creation of shared public value (e.g. access to water, rural electrification, or inclusive education). The creation of diffuse public value is crucial because it provides long-term benefits to society as a whole, not just to a few individuals or groups. This type of value promotes equity and social cohesion, improving the quality of life for all.

The crisis of the liberal international order, accelerated by multipolar dynamics and geopolitical tensions, has weakened the conditions of trust, cooperation, and accountability that enabled public-private partnerships as instruments of global governance. In the absence of a shared value and an institutional framework, PPPs risk losing their effectiveness and legitimacy, exposing the structural limitations already known: imbalance between actors, exclusion of beneficiary communities and opacity of results.

The promise: Collaboration, Scale, and Innovation

To better understand how PPPs contribute to public value creation in the SDGs framework, it is necessary to examine the institutional logic of the SDGs framework itself. Taking a step back, the SDGs are a voluntary global framework that is accepted by signatory nations who commit to "governing through goals" (Pfisterer & Van Tulder, 2020). Thus, political commitments arise for signatories, although there is no possibility of sanctioning states that fail to achieve (or commit to maintain) the stated goals (Mariani et al., 2022). These commitments, accepted by national authorities, have a direct impact on the national bureaucratic machinery. In order to fulfil their commitments, governments are setting up funding and incentive systems for key areas such as education, clean energy, waste management, and inclusive growth. The 17 goals are broken down into 169 indicators, which are reported to the United Nations through the "Global Indicator Framework for the SDGs and Targets of the 2030 Agenda for Sustainable Development" to monitor the status of progress (Ma et al., 2022).

UN guidance consists of general instructions that are part of a universal framework, which then needs to be translated into concrete actions. These actions become granular and go through enabling public hubs at the national, regional and community levels (Haque et al., 2020). In practice, this means that each involved actor should have been equipped with tools and resources over the past 10 years to achieve defined goals. Each of these actors has multiple, non-exclusive roles, such as funding provider, generator, stimulator of innovation and collaboration, including with non-institutional actors, advisor, and promoter of initiatives, capacity building, all geared towards transparency, efficiency, and accountability (Catala et al., 2025; Mariani et al., 2022; Ma et al., 2022; Pfisterer & Van Tulder, 2020). The primary goal is to solve economic, social, and environmental problems by tailoring solutions to different contexts and communities.

More specifically, SDG target 17.16 is dedicated to "*Enhanc[ing] the Global Partnership for Sustainable Development, complemented by multi-stakeholder partnerships that mobilise and share knowledge, expertise, technology and financial resources, to support the achievement of the Sustainable Development Goals in all countries, in particular developing countries*" (United Nation, n.d.). These partnerships represent a fundamental and innovative mechanism that, through knowledge sharing, succeeds in creating stable, diversified and long-term collaborations (Choi et al., 2020, p. 1). These partnerships enable the translation of the global policy framework into concrete actions at the citizen level through coordination and mobilisation of resources (Catala et al., 2025).

The Reality: Imbalance, Exclusion, and Opacity

While PPPs are considered the most suitable instruments for achieving sustainable development goals, they also present problems of imbalance, exclusion, and opacity.

First, as Pfisterer and Van Tulder (2020) point out, a dual logic of governance emerges in PPPs for the SDGs. On one hand, the two actors work in mutual trust and cooperation, sharing power; on the other hand, they do not share the same objectives. This duality creates an **imbalance** that is managed by monitoring and evaluation (M&E) instruments, which have both the task of measuring the achievement of goals and the role of shield and protection when conflicts arise (Ma et al., 2022). This can lead to difficulties in shared leadership and the existence of conflicts of interest and cultural differences where public value intersects with the profit motive (Liu et al., 2024). In addition, the "business risk" of the project should not be transferred to the public actor and, conversely, the private actor cannot be held accountable for failure to achieve social value. There is a need to establish an appropriate risk-sharing mechanism that does not create ambiguity in the roles of the actors involved. Moreover, the driver of inclusiveness, the cornerstone of sustainability, puts the profitability of the involved private sector entity at risk, creating an internal conflict (Catala et al., 2025).

Secondly, the imbalance of this regulation, mitigated by monitoring and evaluation (M&E) systems, leads to an evaluation and reporting perspective which may reflect a lack of attention to the perspectives of the beneficiaries (exclusion). In support of this, the UNECE (United Nations European Commission for Europe) is promoting "People First" PPPs, suggesting a greater awareness to shift the focus on public value creation, observing people and their needs and building partnerships from their perspective. This UNECE call aims to "*explore new ideas and arrangements to improve access to essential services, reduce social inequalities and preserve the environment while transforming the economy*" (Vassileva, 2022, p. 9). This lack of stakeholder management is a critical element from operational shortcomings in public administration and can cause delays in implementation. These shortcomings can be of a regulatory nature or a lack of knowledge on the part of municipalities and local organisations. The risk is the creation of structurally sound and technically perfect partnerships that fail to address the needs of local populations due to the lack of co-design mechanisms.

Finally, one of the main difficulties in achieving the SDGs remains their accountability. This is due to the magnitude of the topic and the lack of internationally measurable, comparable, and universal measurement indicators (Liu et al., 2024). When it comes to PPPs for the SDGs, there is a lack of a clearly and consistently defined fundamental question. Traditional M&E practices are poorly designed to capture social returns, as they are derived from traditional business logic and tend to value short-term tangible outcomes, making it difficult to create social value. Such ambiguous success criteria (opacity) undermine transparency and comparability between projects, confirming the need to find new ways of measuring the effectiveness of these PPPs.

These limitations raise a crucial question: are there alternative partnership models that can ensure inclusive, accountable, and effective implementation of the SDGs? The next section explores the potential of social economy actors in PPPs as a response to these governance challenges.

Digital Social Enterprises: Business Model for Public Value

Hybrid Actors: Mission, Inclusion, and Impact

The crisis of global governance instruments such as PPPs requires alternative models. Social Economy entities emerge as actors capable of bridging this structural gap. Recent literature based on case studies and current projects shows how hybrid actors that combine elements from non-profit organisations (NPO) and for-profit organisations (FPOs) demonstrate higher institutional fit within PPPs. This can be explained by three structural characteristics of hybrid organisations like social enterprises: mission alignment, community inclusion, and impact measurement.

First, these entities embed public value objectives within their social/environmental missions. Unlike traditional public actors, their perspective does not originate from an international system that defines universal objectives. Rather, they operate from a bottom-up perspective, grounded in community needs and context-specific social issues, with a primary focus on generating public value. They adopt a social orientation where collaboration across stakeholder groups is aimed at co-producing social value (Mariani et al., 2022). Many of these social enterprises adopt a formal commitment, integrating SDG objectives into their statutes. This mission-based alignment enables partnerships characterised by shared leadership and joint ownership of objectives. In this case, M&E (minoring & evaluation) systems become collaborative tools not only for monitoring but also for co-designing impact objectives. This facilitates the development of new metrics, especially relevant for assessing progress towards the SDGs. In these realities, mission alignment is not cultural but structural and is a precondition for shared leadership and trust in PPPs.

Secondly, by their very nature, these organisations often emerge from socially committed entrepreneurs who prioritise inclusion and collective benefit by involving beneficiaries in the service design and sometimes in the enterprise itself (as in the case of work cooperatives for marginalised groups). Moreover, their participation in PPPs leads to intrinsic benefits for beneficiaries and broader social groups, as well as extrinsic benefits including dimensions of social, environmental and political value. PPPs involving social enterprises tend to foster closer operational ties with public administrations, enabling more direct engagement with excluded communities (Catala et al., 2025). In addition to the inclusion of beneficiaries, social enterprises actively construct and coordinate multi-actor networks, acting as metagovernors, entities that orchestrate institutional relationships and instruments in the service of collective benefit (Mariani et al., 2022).

Finally, a key distinction in measurement, compared to traditional PPPs, is that social enterprises integrate non-financial performance indicators into their business models, transforming reporting from an external obligation to a structural element of identity. The inclusiveness that results from these types of PPPs builds social trust and legitimacy. They contribute to the design of public policies and are at the forefront of their implementation. Social and environmental metrics are embedded in their missions and operational logic. For social enterprises economic sustainability constitutes a core organisational pillar, minimising reliance on public financial support. In this way, these actors can be regarded as financially autonomous partners, comparable to conventional for-profit firms and often in contrast to traditional nonprofit organisations. As social enterprises are financially stable and self-supporting, they see profit solely as a means to achieve their core objective, social and/or environmental value creation (Mariani et al., 2022; Battilana et al., 2012).

In summary, social enterprises not only bring value coherence and territorial proximity to PPPs for the SDGs, but also help structure more context-sensitive and effective accountability systems. These key elements of social economy actors reframe the perspective of PPPs. If PPPs are created from needs *seen from above*, social enterprises are born from below and from everyday realities. By meeting each other halfway, they can share their knowledge to reach common goals, as envisioned by SDG 17. However, as the complexity of SDG implementation increases - across geographies, sectors, and data systems - even these bottom-up actors face limits in terms of coordination, impact traceability, and scalability.

Digital Social Enterprises Redesign Sustainable Governance

In order to overcome these limitations and achieve the SDGs, a new generation of social enterprises has emerged. As Skivko (2021, p. 168) notes, they "*create social value by applying digital technologies to expand the notion of digital literacy, attract stakeholders, adapt relationships with marginalised groups and effectively communicate the results of this work*". Digital Social Enterprises (DSE) are not traditional social enterprises that adopt digital tools - such as using social networks for advertising. Rather, they integrate digital technologies[1] into their models for creating, measuring and communicating social value, building systemic tools to coordinate multi-level action, track impact in real time and scale interventions across different contexts, radically reinventing the sustainable business model. Digital and social by design, DSEs use technological innovation to manage interdependence, uncertainty, and systemic complexity - key issues in managing sustainable change. They represent a new paradigm of social enterprise, emerging at the intersection of non-profit purpose, business efficiency, and digital innovation (Gregori & Holzmann, 2020), with an emphasis on coordination, impact traceability, and scalability.

First, DSEs tackle the **coordination** challenge by evolving the trust base coordination (typical of social enterprises) into a digital orchestration distributed across stakeholders and geography. Thanks to digital and asynchronous collaboration tools, DSEs increase the efficiency and range of the stakeholder ecosystem, transforming coordination within projects. Thanks to their multi-stakeholder management, uniting different sectors with different operational logics and objectives (public, private, non-profit, etc.) they assume the role of a metagovernor, placing them in the context of technology-enabled social innovation as a bridge between technological innovation and community needs (Battisti, 2019). Their ability to dialogue with governments, organisations and lead users, makes them an ideal hybrid model to exploit technological innovations at the service of sustainable development.

Second, they revolutionise the concept of periodic reporting to embedded real-time accountability. In addition to reporting in an automated way for transparency, these entities use impact-traceability to monitor user needs and to have granular knowledge of the entire value chain (Porter & Kramer, 2006). This is particularly relevant in politically unstable contexts, where needs may shift drastically within hours due to conflict or crisis. Even the provision of support takes place through an exchange of data that is as immediate as possible, overcoming distances and time differences. Reporting is not ex post but is part of the measurement of the business, allowing all the involved actors to intervene and improve efficiency, service, communication and reporting, with the aim of increasing the social impact (Skivko, 2021).

Finally, DSEs amplify the capabilities of social enterprises by becoming globally adaptable and moving away from context dependence. By facilitating the **scalability** of value with digital applications and infrastructures that can be customised according to the needs of communities and countries, Gregori et al. (2020) speak of an "*effortless transferability to other markets*". These innovative entities emerge through a bottom-up approach, evolve into best practices through rigorous data-driven monitoring, and then deploy scalable and customisable top-down solutions across different contexts. In the next section, we will demonstrate the promises of DSEs with real cases of DSE in the SDG context (see the Box 4.1).

Box 4.1 Illustrative Cases of DSEs and their Implications for PPP

This section presents three cases of Digital Social Enterprises[2] (DSEs) that illustrate, in a concrete way, how these actors can respond to the structural limitations of traditional Public-Private Partnerships (PPPs) in the context of the 2030 Agenda. The three examples presented will be analysed and classified according to two theoretical concepts, namely those of Mariani et al. (2022) and Battisti (2019). The objective of this exercise is twofold: to provide empirical evidence of the transformative capacity of DSEs in sustainable development partnerships and to show how they can address the three main limitations of PPPs: imbalance between actors, exclusion of communities and opacity in impact.

The Five Roles of Metagovernor and the Three Typology of Innovations

The first classification framework is that of Mariani et al. (2022), which identifies five operational roles for social economy actors:

- Cultural Spreader: dissemination of the culture of sustainability in the long term, e.g. through conventions or conferences;
- Enabler: enabling connections that collaborate with each other by involving local communities, e.g. by involving citizens in the creation of improvements on the territory;

- Relational Broker: generates innovation by linking resources and roles of different actors, such as indigenous knowledge with advanced research;
- Service Provider: enabler and vehicle of the proposed service, e.g. through a platform;
- Influencer: lobbying capacity for sustainable development, such as a cooperative promoting a regional zero waste law.

These roles allow NPOs to assume the role of a metagovernor, acquiring a specific "*governance that aims to improve the functioning and capacity of relatively self-governing networks to produce governance solutions*" (Mariani et al., 2022, p. 1080). This theoretical framework originated for NPOs but is used here for DSEs. Although NPOs and DSEs are different in their relation to profit, it is suitable for the latter, despite being hybrid and market-oriented. Indeed, they share the mission-driven purpose-oriented creation of public value and furthermore, being digital, they enhance the metagovernance function through their digital capability, scalability, and real-time accountability.

These roles are complemented by the typology of innovation proposed by Battisti (2019) who analyses the innovation process within PPPs. Battisti identifies three levels of technology-driven social innovation and the role of the social entrepreneur in connecting them:

- Internal: composed by innovation managers who share knowledge and *embedded lead-users* (users who use technology with high frequency and are able to give feedback). At this level, the social entrepreneur gets in touch with innovation (technological, organisational, process) and is able to bring it to the other levels interacting with innovation managers and embedded lead-users;
- Open: the social entrepreneur acts as a key resource working with different stakeholders and linking resources through open innovation mechanisms such as contracts or procurement. He enables the partnership;
- Social: composed of members of the community who are strongly technology-oriented and provide feedback on social needs, or promote innovation through online influencing roles. The social entrepreneur acts as a voice for this group by gathering needs and bringing them to the internal level.

SmartICE (Canada) - Internal Innovation/Service Provider/Opacity

SmartICE is a Digital Social Enterprise active in the Canadian Arctic that provides real-time environmental data to Inuit communities through digital sensors and an information platform (SmartICE Monitoring & Information Inc., 2025). The SIKU platform and the SmartBUOY and SmartQAMUTIK are devices that enable continuous monitoring of sea ice, reducing the risk in travel and improving local decision-making capacity. It contributes to SDGs 13[3] and 9[4] by acting as a service provider, creating and delivering data-driven knowledge. At the same time, SmartICE acts mostly at the internal innovation level, discovering and promoting technological innovation to improve resilience for climate change. The project addresses the limit of opacity in environmental PPPs by introducing constant and accessible traceability. The hybrid model combines digital technologies, indigenous knowledge and distributed governance, serving as a concrete example of how DSE can improve measurement and transparency in sustainable development partnerships.

Caare (India) - Open Innovation/Relational Broker/Exclusion

Caare is an Indian Digital Social Enterprise that provides an assisted telemedicine platform that connects rural health workers with urban doctors to provide health services in underserved areas. Digital leverage includes mobile diagnostics, AI (Video Vitals) and institutional interoperability. It addresses the problem of exclusion in health PPPs, which are often unable to engage local actors and address the needs of marginalised communities (Caare, 2025). It contributes to SDGs 3[5] and 10[6] and acts as a relational broker, activating open innovation through a network of stakeholders: communities, public health agencies, technology providers, doctors, and patients. This social business orchestrates adaptive and participatory alliances in complex healthcare contexts.

ElleXX (Switzerland) - Social Innovation/Influencer/Imbalance

Ellexx is a Swiss Digital Social Enterprise addressing gender asymmetries in the economic and financial system. It acts on SDGs 5,[7] 8[8] and 10, playing the role of influencer through an integrated digital platform (ellexx, 2025). Its model combines advice, financial education, investment tools and redistributive membership (one-for-one model) to reduce the gender wealth gap. Ellexx challenges the limit of imbalance, where economic inclusion policies ignore structural biases. Its impact is not only individual but cultural and normative, demonstrating that DSEs can transform power logic through systemic equity-oriented digital infrastructures.

These three cases show how DSEs, while operating outside formal PPP models, directly address some of the structural criticalities that limit the effectiveness of traditional PPPs. This suggests the importance of integrating these hybrid actors within PPPs for sustainable development. The next section explores the concept of the "nexus" between PPPs and DSEs, using these cases as examples and proposing a new operational matrix for SDG governance that aims to serve as a guide for identifying possible partnerships.

DSE–PPP Nexus: A Matrix for Transformative Governance

In order to give continuity to the empirical examples and theoretical references presented so far, this section introduces the concept of the PPP-DSE nexus: a hybrid governance configuration in which Digital Social Enterprises (DSEs) are not mere service providers, but structural enablers of public-private collaboration. This matrix (see Table 4.1) is designed as a guide for the strategic and operational management of partnerships, identifying the contributions of DSEs through different levels of partnership for social value-oriented technological innovation. The aim of this matrix is to categorise social enterprises in order to respond to PPP issues and to enable them as best practices in their different nuances. In this way, best practices and concrete cases can be read with a collaborative strategy-oriented lens. Those presented within the matrix, are cases that, if PPP-enabled, become relational and digitally mediated co-governance ecosystems as well as simple project-oriented tools.

This matrix should not be interpreted as a rigid taxonomy nor as an exhaustive classification.

Rather, it proposes a strategic lens through which to read - and design - the transformative role of Digital Social Enterprises (DSE) within public-private partnerships for sustainable development. Its value lies not in the systematic coverage of possible combinations of limitations and innovations, but in its ability to make visible effective configurations that already exist, showing how certain digital social enterprises already act as infrastructures of distributed governance.

Table. 4.1 PPP-DSE Nexus: Conceptual Matrix Showing How Digital Social Enterprises (DSE) address the Structural Limitations of PPPs (imbalance, exclusion, opacity) through Three Levels of Innovation (Organisational, Collaborative, Institutional). Created by the Authors

PPP Limits →	***Imbalance***	***Exclusion***	***Opacity***
Innovation Level ↓	*Actors in PPP Share Power but Not Share Mission/ Conflicts of Interest and Cultural Differences*	*Lack of Attention to the Perspectives of the Beneficiaries*	*Ambiguous Success Criteria that Undermine Transparency and Comparability*
Internal Manager + embedded lead-users, where digital social entrepreneur get in touch with innovation	*Service Provider* delivering core functions though digital infrastructure; reduces dependency on dominant partners.	*Enabler* provides service to unserved community using accessible technology	*Service provider* offer real-time data for decision-making and public accountability e.g. SmartICE
Open Social entrepreneur + PPP ecosystem, where the partnerships are enabled (open innovation, contracts)	*Relational Broker* aligns institutional and community roles through co-designed platforms	*Relational Broker* enables participatory governance with inclusive digital tools e.g. Caare	*Influencer* Promotes co-created, open-source impact metrics
Social Tech oriented community, where social entrepreneur act as a voice	*Influencer* Redefines power dynamics by advocating for new governance models e.g. ellexx	*Cultural Spreader* Introduce narratives of inclusion and collective agency	*Relational Broker* Builds ecosystems for shared digital transparency and distributed accountability

Each cell of the matrix represents a possible "zone of intervention" where DSEs can activate public value, addressing one of the three structural problems of PPPs (imbalance, exclusion, opacity) through a specific level of innovation (internal, open or social). Operationalising the matrix are the enabling roles: Service Provider, Relational Broker, Enabler, Influencer, and Cultural Spreader. These are not mere labels, but strategic archetypes, which help to reflect on how a social enterprise can act, and with what transformative leverage. The three real-life cases seen above clearly exemplify the usefulness of the matrix:

SmartICE (Canada) fits into the Internal × Opacity cell, as a service provider: a platform that provides real-time environmental data to Inuit communities via sensors and digital tracking. The project addresses the lack of transparency and measurability in environmental PPPs by offering a continuous, natively digital monitoring infrastructure.

Caare (India) represents an example of Open × Exclusion, in the role of Relational Broker. The telemedicine platform connects heterogeneous actors - rural health workers, urban doctors, government agencies, technology providers - to solve health exclusion in marginal areas. It is a case of enabling adaptive and participative alliances in fragile contexts.

elleXX (Switzerland) embodies the Social × Imbalance cell, as Influencer: through a digital financial platform oriented towards women, it intervenes in the structural asymmetries of finance, combining education, ethical investment and redistribution. She not only provides services, but acts as a normative agent, redefining metrics of legitimacy and visibility.

These examples show that the matrix is not a theoretical exercise, but a guide for action. Policy designers can use it to identify where and how to activate DSE strategically in their partnerships. Social entrepreneurs can use it to position their offer, understand their potential hybrid role and build relationships geared towards co-creating public value. For teachers or researchers, the matrix is a teaching tool for analysing real cases and developing systemic reading and transformative design skills. The integration of PPPs and DSEs makes it possible to recover and enhance the three original objectives of PPPs - collaboration, scale, and innovation - by overcoming the structural limitations of traditional partnerships through the digital capabilities and inclusive approach of DSEs.

Finally, it is important to note that some roles - in particular the Enabler - are underrepresented in the matrix, but not because of marginality. On the contrary, the enabling role is often implicitly present in many of the functions observed, acted transversally in contexts where the value does not lie in visibility, but in the ability to make relationships work, enable connections, keep networks active. In this sense, the matrix should be read not only as a map, but as a grammar of transformative action, which helps to orient oneself in the complexity of partnerships for sustainable development, and which recognises in the DSEs not marginal participants, but true architects of digital and inclusive co-governance.

Implications and Open Questions

These cases show that the DSEs already operate as innovation infrastructures, although they are rarely recognised as such within official PPP frameworks. Their integration into SDG-oriented partnerships could open up new paradigms of management, accountability, and collective value creation.

The PPP-DSE nexus is not yet a formalised architecture in international development cooperation. However, the empirical signals and theoretical frameworks indicate that its strategic activation could represent a turning point. As actors capable of crossing sectors, aligning objectives and embedding digital transparency, DSEs can transform PPPs from transactional tools to drivers of transformation. The reviewed limitations of current PPPs for SDGs showed that PPPs can only thrive if they become DSE-compatible. Despite their documented effectiveness in the field, DSEs still face profound barriers to integration into PPPs. For example, procurement systems are designed for large private contractors, not for agile, hybrid companies. Similarly, evaluation metrics penalise complexity and community involvement. DSEs are excluded from decision-making moments, and their digital tools - dashboards, civic apps, impact platforms - are not yet recognised as legitimate public infrastructure. In sum, PPPs are still largely incompatible with the architecture of DSEs unless they reform their institutional logics in depth.

The PPP-DSE nexus is not just a collaboration model: it is a new institutional architecture. For it to become systemic, a change is needed in the way institutions define value, participation, and innovation. Research needs to bridge the conceptual gaps between governance, digital and social impact, exploring emerging models comparatively. On the management side, public managers must acquire digital and relational skills to navigate complex, adaptive, and distributed systems. If PPPs are to remain relevant tools for the future, they must evolve from procurement tools to relational infrastructures: digital, inclusive, and radically transparent. DSEs should not be outsiders to this transformation, they should be its architects. More research is needed.

Conclusion

We conclude by returning to the geopolitical framework outlined in the opening sections. As stated by Acharya (2017), the era of unipolar liberal hegemony is over: today's world is a multiplex system, characterised by multiple, often fragmented and interdependent actors and governance models. In this environment, Public-Private Partnerships (PPPs), born to combine private efficiency and public interest, are losing coherence and legitimacy. Their design and operational logics are proving ill-suited to a global context defined by systemic uncertainty, ecological crisis and institutional distrust.

In this institutional vacuum, new actors are emerging. As shown in this chapter, one such promising new actor is Digital Social Enterprises (DSEs). The promise of DSEs is encapsulated in the fact that next to providing services, they build digital infrastructures of public value, enable distributed participation, and generate models of traceable impact. The matrix proposed in this chapter sought to formalise these diverse contributions, highlighting how DSEs can address the three most critical structural limitations of PPPs - imbalance, exclusion, opacity - through three distinct but integrated levels of innovation: internal, open, and social.

The cases analysed demonstrate that DSEs already operate as hybrid co-governance architectures, although they are not yet recognised in official frameworks. If we want PPPs to remain relevant instruments for the 2030 Agenda, we have to transform them to make them DSE-compatible, as DSEs are not marginal partners but architects of a new relational and transformative infrastructure. The future of sustainable governance therefore depends on our ability to systematically recognise and integrate these promising actors.

Notes

1 The most common technologies are cloud computing, artificial intelligence, 3D printing, mobile computing, ERP systems and Blockchain technology, and more generally online platforms, applications, IOT and ICT (Gregori & Holzmann, 2020).
2 The choice of Social Enterprises was made on the People and Planet First database. People and Planet First is an NPO that map and certify companies that meet six criteria: (I) possess a legal form that protects the long-term purpose, (II) have the purpose of solving social and/or environmental problems, (III) purpose-driven business operations with priority over profit, (IV) operationally demonstrating that purpose drives management choices, (V) have a sustainable and self-sustaining revenue model, and finally, (VI) reinvest the majority of profits in the social purpose.
3 SDGs 13: Climate action.
4 SDGs 9: Industry, innovation and infrastructure.
5 SDGs 3: Good health and well-being.
6 SDGs 10: Reduced inequalities.
7 SDGs 5: Gender equality.
8 SDGs 8: Decent work and economic growth.

References

Acharya, A. (2017). After Liberal Hegemony: The Advent of a Multiplex World Order. *Ethics & International Affairs*, *31*(3), 271–285. Retrieved 5 2, 2025, from https://doi.org/10.1017/S089267941700020X

Battilana, J., Lee, M., Walker, J., & Dorsey, C. (2012). In Search of the Hybrid Ideal. *Stanford Social Innovation Review*, 51–55. Retrieved 5 2, 2025, from https://ssir.org/articles/entry/in_search_of_the_hybrid_ideal

Battisti, S. (2019). Digital Social Entrepreneurs as Bridges in Public–Private Partnerships. *Journal of Social Entrepreneurship*, *10*(2), 135–158. Retrieved 5 2, 2025, from https://doi.org/10.1080/19420676.2018.1541006

Biggeri, M., Bortolotti, L., Saccone, D., & Tassinari, M. (2023). Policy and Political Challenges for a Better World: The United States and China Pathways towards the 2030 Agenda. *Ecological Economics*, *209*(1–4). https://doi.org/10.1016/j.ecolecon.2023.107821

Caare. (2025). *Speciality care*. Retrieved 05 14, 2025, from https://caare.in/

Catala, B., Savall, T., & Chaves-Avila, R. (2025, January 14). Social Economy and Public Private Partnerships: Analysis, Drivers, and Prospects from the Local Level for Territorial Development. *Nonprofit Policy Forum*, *2025*, 1–24. https://doi.org/10.1515/npf-2024-0020

Choi, G., Jin, T., Jeong, Y., & Kyoung Lee, S. (2020). Evolution of Partnerships for Sustainable Development: The Case of P4G. *Sustainability*, *12*(16), 6485. Retrieved 5 2, 2025, from https://doi.org/10.3390/su12166485

Deudney, D., & Ikenberry, G. J. (1999). The Nature and Sources of Liberal International Order. *Review of International Studies*, *25*(2), 179–196. Retrieved 5 2, 2025, from https://doi.org/10.1017/S0260210599001795

ellexx. (2025). *Die Finanzplattform für Frauen*. Retrieved 05 14, 2025, from https://www.ellexx.com/de/

Gregori, P., & Holzmann, P. (2020, November). Digital Sustainable Entrepreneurship: A Business Model Perspective on Embedding Digital Technologies for Social and Environmental Value Creation. *Journal of Cleaner Production*, *272*, 122817. https://doi.org/10.1016/j.jclepro.2020.122817

Haque, M. N., Saroar, M., Fattah, M. A., & Morshed, S. R. (2020, December 12). Public-Private Partnership for Achieving Sustainable Development Goals: A Case Study of Khulna, Bangladesh. *Public Administration and Policy*, *23*, 283–298. https://doi.org/10.1108/PAP-04-2020-0023

Ikenberry, G. J. (2025). Liberalism, Institutional Statecraft, and International Order. In T. V. Paul, A. Wivel, & K. He (Eds.), *International Organizations and Peaceful Change in World Politics* (1st ed., pp. 55–77). Cambridge University Press. Retrieved May 5, 2025, from https://doi.org/10.1017/9781009509367.005

Liu, L. X., Clegg, S. R., & Pollack, J. (2024). What Have We Learnt about PPPs? In *Handbook on Public–Private Partnerships in International Infrastructure Development* (pp. 467–506). Edward Elgar Publishing. https://www.elgaronline.com/view/book/9781839102769/book-part-9781839102769-26.xml

Ma, M., Wang, N., Mu, W., & Zhang, L. (2022, October 24). The Instrumentality of Public-Private Partnerships for Achieving Sustainable Development Goals. *Sustainability*. 13756. https://doi.org/10.3390/su142113756

Mariani, L., Trivellato, B., Martini, M., & Mariafioti, E. (2022, November). Achieving Sustainable Development Goals through Collaborative Innovation: Evidence from Four European Initiatives. *Journal of Business Ethics*, *180*, 1075–1095. https://doi.org/10.1007/s10551-022-05193-z

Meier, D. S. (2023). The Evolution of SDG-Related Third Sector and Public Administration Literature: An Analysis and Call for More SDG-Related Research. *Sustainability: Science, Practice and Policy*, *19*(1), 2236501. Retrieved 5 2, 2025, from https://doi.org/10.1080/15487733.2023.2236501

National Immigrant Justice Center. (2025, January 22). *Leading with Cruelty: Eight Impacts of Trump's First Day Executive Orders Author NIJC Staff*. Retrieved 5 6, 2025, from https://immigrantjustice.org/staff/blog/leading-cruelty-eight-impacts-trumps-first-day-executive-orders

People and Planet First. (2025). Verified Enterprise Directory. *Global Directory of People and Planet First Verified Enterprises*. Retrieved 05 20, 2025, from https://verified.peopleandplanetfirst.org/directory

Pfisterer, S., & Van Tulder, R. (2020, December 24). Navigating Governance Tensions to Enhance the Impact of Partnerships with the Private Sector for the SDGs. *Sustainability*, *13*(1), 111. https://doi.org/10.3390/su13010111

Porter, M. E., & Kramer, M. R. (2006, December). The Link Between Competitive Advantage and Corporate Social Responsibility. *Harvard Business Review*, *84*, 78–92.

Quaye, J. N. A., Halsall, J. P., Winful, E. C., Snowden, M., Opuni, F. F., Hyams-Ssekasi, D., Afriyie, E. O., Opoku-Asante, K., Ocloo, E. C., & Fairhurst, B. (2024). Social Enterprises and the Sustainable Development Goals (SDGs): A Means to an End. *Springer - Environment, Development and Sustainability*. Retrieved 5 2, 2025, from https://doi.org/10.1007/s10668-024-05359-x

Skivko, M. (2021, December 01). Digital Technologies, Social Entrepreneurship and Governance for Sustainable Development. *Research in Social Change 13*, 165–173. https://doi.org/10.2478/rsc-2021-0016

SmartICE Monitoring & Information Inc. (2025). Enabling Resiliency in the Face of Climate Change. *SmartICE*. Retrieved 5 12, 2025, from https://smartice.org/

United Nation Department of Economic and Social Affairs. (n.d.). Goal 17 Strengthen the means of implementation and revitalize the Global Partnership for Sustainable Development.

Vassileva, A. (2022, November 19). Green Public-Private Partnerships (PPPs) as an Instrument for Sustainable Development. *Journal of World Economy: Transformations & Transitions*, *2*(05), 22. https://doi.org/10.52459/jowett25221122

Tools

ChatGPT version 3.5, OpenAI: openai.com/chat. Helping with creation of text structure.

DeepL Translate, Deepl SE: deepl.com/translator. Translation of text passages.

NotebookLM, Google: notebooklm.google.com. Literature research, creation of summaries.

5 Digital Social Entrepreneurship

Technological Implications of Scaling and Inclusive Approaches for Disadvantaged Entrepreneurs

Alan Martin and Alan Murray

Introduction: The Digital Transformation of Social Entrepreneurship

Social entrepreneurship is recognised as being an important and effective approach to addressing complex societal challenges that traditional public sector interventions or market-based solutions have failed to adequately resolve (Austin et al., 2006; Bacq & Janssen, 2011). In the last decade, digital technologies have revolutionised the field of social entrepreneurship, leading to the creation of what is now termed "digital social entrepreneurship" (DSE). This is essentially the utilisation of digital technologies to create, scale and sustain social ventures (Prodanov, 2018) and this transformation is occurring within a wider context of what is often termed the Fourth Industrial Revolution, exemplified by the growth of automation, artificial intelligence, and increasing digital connectivity. Collectively this is currently reshaping and reimagining our existing economic structures and social relations (Sahai & Rath, 2021)

DSE represents the intersection of two very dynamic fields: social entrepreneurship with its focus on addressing social problems through the creation of innovative business models and digital entrepreneurship, the harnessing and leveraging of emerging technologies to create or transform business ventures (Nambisan, 2017). (Rengaraju et al., 2024) state that the advent of digital technologies and the proliferation of online platforms have transformed how social enterprises operate, scale, and deliver impact. This represents a convergence that has brought unprecedented opportunities to address social challenges, whilst simultaneously raising questions about access, inclusion, and the distribution of benefits.

It should be noted, however, that digitalisation of social entrepreneurship is not simply about the adoption of new and emerging tools; instead it constitutes a seismic shift in the social value that can potentially be created, delivered, and ultimately, scaled. These technologies enable social entrepreneurs to reach and obtain larger audiences, gather and interrogate data effectively, mobilise and deploy their resources more efficiently and

DOI: 10.4324/9781003583448-6

grow and scale impact in ways that, until now, were impossible (Özman & Gossart, 2024). Simultaneously, these technologies can compound existing inequalities if those disadvantaged groups lack capital, skills or infrastructure to access them (Orser et al., 2019).

Understanding Digital Social Entrepreneurship

Definitions and Key Characteristics

DSE symbolises the merging point of social entrepreneurship and digital technologies and the coming together of the mission-driven orientation of social ventures with the transformational opportunities and potential of digital tools and platforms. DSE adds a technological dimension simultaneously enabling and transforming social entrepreneurial endeavour and activity. DSE can further be defined as the application of digital technologies to create sustainable solutions to unaddressed problems (Ghalwash et al., 2017). This includes undertakings that leverage digital platforms, tools and ecosystems to create, deliver, and scale social value. Prodanov (2018) states that digital technologies support the collaboration of people and the sharing of resources across the globe, freeing the social entrepreneur from the limitations of time and space. They allow funds to be raised, resources to be pooled and effort to be shared at local, national, and international level in the pursuit of specific social goals.

The attributes of DSE reflect the distinctive capabilities that digital technologies contribute to social value creation. The use of platform-based value creation appears to offer a distinct shift from the traditional value chains to more multi-sided and sophisticated platforms that are designed to increase stakeholder connectivity. Their aim is to drive value creation through creating better user interactions as opposed to a more linear production (Muzellec et al., 2015). Through this type of transformation innovative social enterprises have been presented with the opportunity to facilitate valuable interactions and collaborations amongst increasingly diverse groups of stakeholders. This, in turn, has enabled value network creation that has extended far beyond that which more traditional independent players could have potentially hoped to achieve.

Increasingly data-driven decision making has become another trait of DSEs, where increased usage of the potential of data collection, analysis, and visualisation is harnessed to inform strategy, measure impact and demonstrate organisational value to stakeholders (Özman & Gossart, 2024). Utilisation of evidence-based approaches in social problem-solving has enabled organisations to adjust and adapt their efforts using real-time feedback and further empirical evidence of what works in varying contexts.

The powerful impact of network effects that digital social ventures can leverage can potentially accelerate their impact, with value creation growing as service users continue to join their platforms (Braund & Schwittay, 2016). This propagates cyclical growth that can aid rapid expansion of reach and effectiveness of social interventions, however, conversely it can also promote a "winner-takes-all" dynamic which attributes power to the most successful platforms.

DSE scaling can also be facilitated by the economics of digital technologies enabling lower marginal costs compared to traditional organisations. Digital enterprises predominantly have high fixed costs, but lower marginal costs, thus enabling social ventures to serve additional users at negligible additional expense once the infrastructure has been established (Prodanov, 2018). This fundamental economic characteristic alters the financial modelling of social impact, with the potential to allow successful DSEs to obtain significant scale without a directly proportionate increase in resources.

A growing lack of geographically structured boundaries has emerged as another key characteristic. DSEs increasingly, and more easily, undertake operations across many geographic boundaries when contrasted with more traditional social enterprises who may not have the capability to undertake these activities. Issues of cultural, regulatory, and contextual differences remain areas that this type of organisation are still required to navigate (Özman & Gossart, 2024). This cross-border capability has released incredible new potential for addressing global challenges and the development of solution sharing across contexts, whilst also creating the ability to undertake meaningful conversation and debate about the consideration of cultural sensitivity and local adaptation.

Finally, usage of digital platforms stimulates and facilitates unprecedented activity in co-creation and open innovation throughout a diverse range of stakeholders, enabling more inclusive and participatory approaches to solving social challenges (Khajeheian & Friedrichsen, 2017). Collaborative capability can facilitate democratic innovation processes ensuring appropriate solutions are developed with, rather than for, the communities they aim to serve.

Types of Digital Social Enterprises

DSEs manifest themselves in many different ways which is a direct reflection of the diversity of the technologies that can be brought to bear when trying to address social challenges. Building on the taxonomies offered by researchers such as Özman and Gossart (2024) and Ghalwash et al. (2017), several distinct categories can be identified that demonstrate both the breadth and versatility of a digital approach to social innovation.

An important category in this field involves platforms that specialise in civic engagement who have the specific aim of increasing civic participation, transparency, and democratic engagement through the utilisation of digital tools. This can include participatory budget creation, policy co-creation and civic monitoring of public services. Examples of this type of organisation include Decide Madrid, a Spanish participatory democracy platform, and FixMyStreet, which allows UK citizens to highlight very specific local issues to participating local authorities (Özman & Gossart, 2024). These platforms allow appropriate technologies to be leveraged with the aim of strengthening democratic processes and increasing a citizen's ability to participate in the process of governance, seeking to address the challenges raised by the growing perception of political disengagement and lack of transparency in public decision-making processes.

Initiatives that are focused on data access and transparency centre on the collection, analysis, and visualisation of data to address social and environmental challenges such as platforms like OpenCorporate whose role is to provide open data on corporations worldwide with the aim of promoting corporate transparency and accountability (Özman & Gossart, 2024). By taking, analysing, and then transforming previously inaccessible, or often fragmented information; into a state that is both readily available and easily usable, this type of initiative facilitates better informed decision-making and advocacy which, in turn, empowers organisations and citizens to hold more powerful organisations to account.

New digital inclusion platforms have the very specific objective of targeting action on the digital divide by enabling technology access and skills development and creating suitable opportunities for communities that are otherwise marginalised. These include programs that offer affordable access to digital devices and internet connectivity, as well as training programs for digital literacy. An example of this would be Reconnect (formerly WeFarm) who provide digital information services to smallholder farmers who do not have internet access using SMS-based knowledge sharing systems (Rahman et al., 2017). This example illustrates how, through the adaptation of technology, existing infrastructure constraints can be overcome bringing tangible benefits for the community of users.

Collaborative economy platforms have made it their mission to create a more efficient digital environment enabling sustainable peer-to-peer exchanges, easing the sharing of Information and fostering increased user collaboration. They seek to use the effects of the influence of distributed resources to drive community cooperation in pursuit of their goal of generating increased social value. For example grassroot community who are group of people that work together and are empowered by the use of digital technologies (Fu et al., 2025). The aim here is to jointly tackle environmental sustainability and address food security challenges by using market-based mechanisms to bring together committed stakeholders from the sector with users who, ultimately, gain social value from these efforts.

Platforms that offer digital health and welfare solutions are using digital technologies to improve health outcomes and individual's welfare, with their emphasis typically on isolated and underserved populations. Examples of this type of platform would include telemedicine sites for remote areas, digital health tools for individuals suffering from more chronic conditions and platforms that can act as an interface to connect social services to vulnerable people. The DSE DoctHers get together female healthcare providers, offering digital health consulting services to widen access to this industry.

Allowing more ready access to financial products through the creation of alternative digital finance platforms can help to democratise access to finance through the use of techniques like crowdfunding, or peer-to-peer lending and even digital microfinance, again with the central aim of delivering social impact. An example of this type of social enterprise is Kiva who play a key role in connecting lenders with entrepreneurs in developing countries. Another example of this type of social enterprise is Goteo who specialise in providing crowdfunding and specifically target projects with open source and social impact facets (Braund & Schwittay, 2016). Platforms like this aim to address the traditional obstacles to financial inclusion whilst also trying to maintain a focus on social outcomes placing these values ahead of commercial returns.

Digital skills and education sites can utilise appropriate technologies to widen access to a quality education and foster skills development, particularly for disadvantaged groups. This type of social venture typically includes those who offer online courses, virtual mentoring, and skills verification designed for more marginalised groups. An example of this is Laboratoria who offers training for women from low-income households in Latin America, providing them with the skills to become web developers and then connecting them with suitable work opportunities (Martínez-Restrepo & Gray, 2020). This approach has been shown to successfully tackle both gender and skills inequality gaps in the technology sector.

Scaling Strategies and Approaches

A central concern for social entrepreneurs is scaling social impact to adequately address complex societal challenges effectively. As Islam (2022) notes, in the context of social enterprises, scaling social impact is considered to be the main currency or a key performance metric. Digital technologies have led to the emergence of new scaling possibilities, along with new challenges and considerations. Research in this field has identified three distinct but complementary strategies: scaling out, scaling up, and scaling deep (Özman & Gossart, 2024; Moore et al., 2015; Westley et al., 2014). Each of these is, in turn, affected by digital technologies in a different way, creating unique opportunities and constraints for DSEs.

Scaling Out: Expanding Reach and Replication

The term "scaling out" refers to the process by which a social enterprise seeks to expand its reach and impact by establishing itself in new locations, markets or contexts (Moore et al., 2015). This expansion obviously brings with it a rise in the level of customers served and a subsequent expansion of the social enterprise in organisational terms which can often be in the form of franchising or the formation of new business units (Islam, 2022). This is a tried and tested approach in the field of social entrepreneurship and indeed the measure of scaling success is often the number of beneficiaries served. Network effects bring benefits to the digital user around scaling out as user and member numbers increase without the need for higher levels of investment in technology (Braund & Schwittay, 2016).

Prodanov (2018) suggests that, in some ways, the financial benefits to the DSE are greatest where a scaling out approach is adopted as once the basic infrastructure has been developed the cost of reaching and serving the community it is serving becomes cost effective and facilitates international growth as digital networks are not generally inhibited by geographical boundaries. Indeed, taking the example of education, algorithms, and digital technologies can now ensure that online content and delivery can be standardised anywhere in the world which has clear benefits in terms of consistency (Özman & Gossart, 2024) even though this is achieved at the cost of local contextualisation. Furthermore, uneven distribution of access to appropriate digital technologies can cause problems when scaling out as not everyone has access to these enabling technologies (Orser et al., 2019). This effect is particularly evident in disadvantaged sectors (Özman & Gossart, 2024, p. 57).

According to Uvin et al. (2000) additional challenges also exist such as the elevation of growth metrics over social impact as a priority. This creates a clear issue for the social enterprise. as organisational growth and social impact are not the same thing. DSEs must stay true to their social mission and social objectives and ensure impact in these areas is not reduced by expansion ambitions. In the same vein an over dependence on digital platforms can leave the social enterprise vulnerable and exposed as users become caught up in power dynamics around who controls the flow of data. This raises additional questions around long term sustainability (Gümüsay et al., 2020).

Scaling Up: Transforming Systems and Institutions

The term "scaling up" relates to efforts to address complex social problems by transforming policy, processes and organisations (Moore et al., 2015). Scaling up is concerned not with the development of a single organisation but is instead focussed on the shaping and reforming of the wider ecosystem in order to create a culture of social innovation (Westley & Antadze, 2010). This recognises that sustainable social change regularly needs change at the systemic level rather than just at an individual or organisational level.

Digital technological innovations are transforming how social enterprises approach scaling up in a number of important ways. Data-powered advocacy enables social enterprises to collect, analyse, and visualise data about social problems in numerous new ways that can strongly inform advocacy efforts (Charalabidis et al., 2016). An example of this in practice is OpenCorporates which makes data on corporations open and freely available but also supports "data-based advocacy" aimed at promoting Corporates to be transparent in their policies (Özman & Gossart, 2024). This data-driven approach supports transparency and evidence based decision making for policymakers and the public alike.

Technology transfer and open source approaches enable digital social enterprises to scale up through sharing their technological innovations to others, particularly through open-source licensing and collaborative development models (Bhatt et al., 2016). As Özman and Gossart (2024) note, by making these technologies available to all this then supports the development of an ecosystem and improves the effectiveness of efforts as different actors are able to work on the same problem together with reduced barriers. Undertaking technological diffusion by this method can multiply impact beyond what a single organisation may achieve, creating systemic capacity for addressing social challenges.

Digital network building represents another meaningful mechanism to aid scaling up as digital platforms enable new forms of collaboration and coalition-building transcending traditional boundaries and facilitating a collective action for systemic change (Westley et al., 2014). Social media, collaborative workspace areas and technology based communication tools simplify the coordination of diverse stakeholders around shared goals, unlocking the potential to accelerate institutional change processes by the reduction of coordination costs and allowing more efficient information sharing.

The creation of digital public goods and assets - non-competitive, non-excludable digital resources that can benefit many across entire ecosystems - represents a different approach to scaling up in the digital context (McGann et al., 2018). Access to open data initiatives, shared protocols and collaborative knowledge bases can create value that can extend far beyond direct users and consumers of a specific service, building commons-based resources that support broad-based social innovation.

However, there are some challenges associated with using digital approaches to scale up which must be considered. The level of technical expertise and resources needed to undertake the technically complex processes in creating these technologies that can be effectively adopted by diverse organisations is not insignificant (Prodanov, 2018). As a result numerous social enterprises struggle to develop robust, adaptable digital solutions that can be easily implemented by others across different contexts and organisational capacities. Governance tensions are also a factor around open source and collaborative approaches, bringing to the fore questions of a complex nature about decision-making, resource allocation and accountability (Gümüsay et al., 2020). Digital literacy gaps are a limiting factor in the diffusion of digital social innovations, as many potential adopters may lack the technical capacity to effectively implement available technologies (Orser et al., 2019). Finally, digital technologies can further entrench pre-existing power dynamics rather than having a role in transforming them if access to and control over these technologies remains concentrated among a few already-privileged actors (Martinez Dy et al., 2018).

Scaling Deep: Transforming Relationships and Culture

The term "scaling deep" refers to the goal of transforming community relationships, networks, values and perceptions (Moore et al., 2015). Deploying this approach highlights that sustainable social change requires shifts in how people perceive and understand problems, relate to each other, and engage with and within their communities. As Westley et al. (2014) note, scaling deep involves the process of changing hearts and minds, not just structures and systems. This dimension of scaling is often found to be more challenging but also the most critical for creating lasting social transformation.

Digital technologies offer DSEs new possibilities and challenges for scaling deep. Digital community building through online platforms can facilitate community formation around shared interests and values seeking commonalities, whilst having the potential to create a space for transformative dialogue and relationship building (Allen & Light, 2015). Digital communities are largely unconstrained and can transcend geographic limitations while still trying to foster meaningful connections and shared identity, enabling people to seek out and find others who share their values and commitments even when they are geographically divergent.

Experiential digital learning tools, which can include interactive simulations, virtual or augmented reality experiences, and serious games, can also create immersive learning experiences that can alter perspectives and help to grow and build empathy more effectively than traditional information-based approaches (Raybourn, 2014). These technologies enable people to experience different perspectives and situations in new ways that can act as a catalyst to help change attitudes and values, potentially accelerating and driving the cultural transformation processes that scaling deep seeks and often requires.

The opportunities for peer-to-peer knowledge exchange that is facilitated by digital platforms can democratise the process of knowledge sharing by enabling horizontal learning among peers, challenging more traditional expert-novice situations and hierarchies and validating diverse forms of knowledge (Rahman et al., 2017). This process of democratisation can empower communities to develop and deliver their own solutions whilst building their confidence in their own capabilities, developing the sense of agency and self-efficacy that is a prerequisite for deeper cultural change.

Amongst the more effective approaches to scaling deep is to combine online and offline engagement, using digital tools to augment and complement traditional approaches rather than replace face-to-face interaction (Özman & Gossart, 2024). For example, civic engagement platforms may facilitate online discussion while also enabling the organisation of local physical gatherings to foster and deepen user relationships and commitment, recognising that to create lasting cultural change requires both the reach that digital tools provide as well as the depth that personal relationships enable.

The process of scaling deep through digital methods faces particular challenges that DSEs have to carefully navigate their way through. Digital distancing remains a fundamental tension, as emerging digital technologies are fundamentally about "killing the distance" (Özman & Gossart, 2024, p. 59), potentially undermining the deeper human connections required for transformative learning and relationship establishment and building. The convenience and efficiency of digital interaction may highlight potential costs including the vulnerability and intimacy that deeper cultural or social change requires.

Technological isolation also poses a significant risk, as DSEs may become "encapsulated in technological bubbles isolated from other actors operating in real life, which eventually undermines their capacity to reach the social goals they aim for" (Özman & Gossart, 2024, p. 59). Remaining grounded in lived realities and shared experiences whilst maintaining connections to offline communities is ultimately essential for effective scaling deep. Additionally, scaling deep requires what Schot and Steinmueller (2018) call "second-order learning" - changing worldviews, values, and identities in the process. Digital environments may not always be able to support the vulnerability, trust, and sustained engagement needed for this type of transformative learning to happen.

Finally, there is a tendency of digital platforms and solutions to create filter bubbles and echo chambers through the processes of algorithmic filtering and homophilous network formation (Pariser, 2011) which runs counter to the objective of the transformation of perspectives and building bridges across societal differences. DSEs must try to actively work in countering these tendencies and aim to create platforms that can facilitate meaningful encounters between individuals with numerous different perspectives and worldviews.

Balancing Multiple Scaling Strategies

It is useful to understand and distinguish between scaling out, up, and deep as distinct strategies, effective DSEs can often employ varying combinations of these approaches. Each strategy addresses different aspects of social change, therefore integrating these approaches can potentially create more comprehensive and sustainable impacts. Research by Özman and Gossart (2024) discovered that DSEs sit within three broad types based on their scaling orientations, each one highlighting different combinations of these.

The *grassroots orientation* cluster primarily focuses on scaling deep through facilitating physical exchanges, local revival activities, training, and mentoring. These platforms focus on and enhance the process of community building and transforming relationships and practices, recognising that sustainable and long lasting social change can require deep cultural shifts within communities. Organisations within this cluster can typically prioritise the quality of user engagement over the total quantity of users, investing in mechanisms that support relationship building and shared and mutual learning among their participants.

The *technology solution* cluster focuses their efforts on scaling up by providing appropriate technologies that other organisations can then further adapt and use, often delivered through open-source methods. These platforms place the emphasis on ecosystem building and fostering institutional change, recognising that their greatest potential impact comes from the enablement of other organisations to become more effective rather than directly serving end beneficiaries. This particular approach requires more significant technical capabilities but can deliver results by achieving broader systemic impact by building and growing the technological infrastructure that can foster and support widespread social innovation.

The *data-based growth* cluster aligns its focus on scaling out through global reach, data crowdsourcing, and the impact of network effects. These platforms place their emphasis upon efficient replication and expansion, leveraging all the potential economic advantages of digital technologies to try to achieve massive scale. Organisations found in this cluster would typically prioritise their user growth and geographic expansion, using all available data and algorithms to optimise their chosen services for the broadest appeal to generate viral growth.

Each type faces a different set of scaling challenges and requires different internal capabilities to achieve this. Most importantly, existing research suggests that digital technologies do not necessarily lead to a given scaling pathway. Instead, strategic choices about how to leverage digital tools ultimately shape which scaling strategies present as the most feasible and effective. As Islam (2020) noted, there exists tensions between different scaling approaches, with scaling out potentially undermining scaling deep when organisational growth outpaces the development of substantive relationships and real cultural change. DSEs must attempt to navigate these tensions carefully, having to consider how their own unique technological choices could either facilitate or hinder the different dimensions of scaling. The most successful digital social enterprises could be those that can dynamically balance the multiple scaling strategies, adapting their approach based on context, opportunity and impact objectives responding to emergent challenges as they occur.

Inclusivity and Barriers for Disadvantaged Entrepreneurs

Whilst digital technologies undoubtedly offer huge possibilities for the social entrepreneur, if they are not utilised strategically in order to maximise inclusivity they can actually create new barriers to uptake which can be detrimental to the social aim of the social enterprise. This requests the development of scaling diversification that allows to address different Sustainable Development Goals along with Scaling by Bridging Complementary Institutional Voids in order to compensate where institutional regulation and support fail. In turn, it is connected with the limits and disadvantages emerged from the use of technologies. For instance, the concept of the "digital divide" has evolved over time from having a focus on physical access to technology to a much more nuanced understanding of the multiple and varying dimensions of digital inequality (Graham, 2011). For entrepreneurs, with particular regard to those from disadvantaged backgrounds, these inequalities can manifest themselves in several interconnected ways that create complex and compounded barriers to their active participation in the digital economy. Infrastructure access continues to be a fundamental challenge, with basic digital infrastructure continuing to be unevenly distributed. Rural, low-income and marginalised communities remain amongst those who often have limited, low or poor-quality access to broadband and internet access as well as reliable electricity (UNCTAD, 2014). This is a fundamental inequality that constrains the ongoing ability of entrepreneurs from within these communities to participate fully and constructively in the digital economy, limiting their access to online markets, digital tools and virtual networks that are increasingly becoming essential tools for entrepreneurial success. Beyond infrastructure, device availability is a relevant and major issue with access to appropriate modern devices like computers, smartphones, and tablets with sufficient capabilities to run current software is not universal (Ameen & Willis, 2016). Those disadvantaged entrepreneurs may have limited devices or devices that are obsolete with outdated specifications that impose restrictions on what digital tools they can run or effectively use, vastly constraining and, ultimately, limiting their ability to leverage potentially advanced digital capabilities for their ventures. However, perhaps the most persistent dimension of the digital divide is related to gender.

An individual's gender signifies one of the most well-documented dimensions of inequality in digital entrepreneurship. Orser et al.'s (2019) research identifies that specific gender-rated barriers to technology adoption that are faced by female entrepreneurs, subsequently create further challenges for women seeking to utilise and leverage digital technologies in social entrepreneurship ventures. A foundational challenge is represented by gaps in knowledge and exposure, as women often gain less exposure to technology from early years, which, in turn, leads to knowledge gaps that may persist into their entrepreneurial careers. Women often have less technological knowledge and this can severely limit IT adoption amongst female entrepreneurs. These gaps arise from gendered patterns in the education system, in particular in STEM (Science, Technology, Engineering, and Mathematics) based fields, compounded by differing socialisation experiences with technology that can begin as far back as childhood and carry on through formal education and early career experiences. Women face an additional barrier around their own perceptions of their digital capabilities which can limit digital uptake amongst female entrepreneurs. The research shows they are less comfortable around technology in a business context and can be less competent as a result. This lack of digital confidence can create a negative cycle where, for the female entrepreneur, technology is avoided and the opportunities it offers are missed (Mack et al., 2017). Such constraints are also often interconnected as those women who are managing busy family lives and responsibilities are likely to have less time to invest in their personal development to acquire the knowledge needed to operate and understand new technologies, whilst those suffering from limited financial resources cannot hope to afford professional technology support. The gender bias often found in technology support systems can further exacerbate and create additional systemic barriers. The supporting ecosystem for digital entrepreneurship often exhibits in-built gender bias in their design, culture, and future implementation.

Barriers for other Disadvantaged Groups

Clearly gender has been the focus of a significant amount of research around inequality however other dimensions of disadvantage can also create significant barriers to participation in DSE. These barriers often intersect with gender, creating compounded challenges for entrepreneurs with potentially multiple marginalised identities. An individual's age can cause barriers, in particular for older entrepreneurs who can often face digital challenges that relate to both skills and perceptions. The work of Kusumaningtyasa and Suwartob (2015) highlights that age correlates with technology adoption rates, where older entrepreneurs are generally found to be less technology savvy and therefore are more likely to delegate those tasks which are technology based to others. In the rapidly changing world of digital technologies this creates particular challenges where continuous personal development is a critical facet of the ambitious entrepreneur. More mature entrepreneurs can also face age discrimination in both technology support programs and network based events that often assume a younger demographic, thus limiting their access to potential learning opportunities and valuable peer support. Further constraints and barriers are present which centre around socio-economic origins, specifically those from low-income backgrounds. This creates a multiplicity of intersecting constraints which include limited financial resources for technology investment, decreased exposure due to educational background to appropriate technologies and typically more limited social networks with relevant digital and technological expertise (Rahman et al., 2017). The compounded effect of these barriers for socio-economically challenged entrepreneurs is to create significant obstacles to DSE as they must navigate to try and overcome these multiple shortfalls simultaneously while operating with fewer resources when contrasted with more affluent peers. Geography also has a part to play for entrepreneurs from more rural contexts who face distinct challenges that typically include limited infrastructure access, fewer in-person technology training opportunities and considerably smaller local networks with appropriate digital expertise (UNCTAD, 2014). Entrepreneurs in a rural context may also face cultural barriers if DSE is felt to be incompatible with those rural values or lifestyles. It has been noted that challenges which are geographical in nature have the potential to be addressed by digital tools thus reducing isolation effects however the reverse effect can be seen where users are unable to access digital resources and therefore are unable to participate. Similar social exclusion has been seen to take place where the user has challenges around digital literacy as a result of educational gaps (Erumi-Esin & Heeks, 2015), a phenomenon which is often observed in low income communities. Both technical and social obstacles are often faced by those with disabilities leading to a lack of participation in DSE creation. Entrepreneurs facing disability often have to overcome obstacles ranging from inaccessible digital tools to support programs that rarely address the unique needs of disabled entrepreneurs (United Nations, 2019). Whilst there are any number of digital platforms which could add value to the enterprise these are often inaccessible to users with various and unique disabilities, while support programs can compound the issue by failing to provide appropriate accommodation to facilitate meaningful participation by disabled entrepreneurs. This is a particular issue in so much as the potential of digital technologies to create and develop inclusive solutions to problems can be harnessed if the design processes favour inclusivity. Immigrant entrepreneurs have been identified as a particularly disadvantaged group in the context of DSEs as they are often isolated and excluded by the wider society and lack the necessary support networks needed to develop their digital capabilities (David & Terstriep, 2025). This group is also exposed to discrimination and high levels of bureaucracy which again can make accessing the digital economy challenging (David & Terstriep, 2025). Within this constraint it has been found that gender is even more likely to contribute to the digital divide, with migrant women facing inequality in access to infrastructure, attainment of digital skills development and gender-blind digital technology interventions that may, unconsciously, exclude their participation (Drydakis, 2024). Further constraints exist due to language and information gaps which can lead to access to institutional support, grants, and funding and business development services, with many immigrant entrepreneurs reporting a low awareness of DSE resources (David & Terstriep, 2025). Furthermore, limited social capital and network access can restrict their ability to form strategic partnerships, access mentorship, and secure funding - all of which are critical resources for scaling DSE innovations (Suseno & Abbott, 2021). According to David and Terstriep (2025) these additional challenges faced by immigrant entrepreneurs can limit their effectiveness and stifle their potential.

Immigrant entrepreneurs face a broad set of challenges as previously discussed, they, therefore, require a multi-dimensional approach to address these structural, social, and technological barriers. Cross-sector collaboration emerges as a critical and vital strategy, with research demonstrating the importance of the engagement of multiple and diverse stakeholder groups that include governments, the private sector and civil society in a participatory process of co-creation the gives a sense of empowerment immigrant entrepreneurs to help shape initiatives instead of simply being the benefactors of schemes created in their absence. Digital technologies, it has been shown, have a dual role in the context of inclusivity facilitation by embodying social innovation through technology-enabled solutions and acting as a platform for enablement of broader social innovation amongst women and marginalised entrepreneurs (Suseno & Abbott, 2021). Pivotal to the success is developing of culturally responsive strategic communications, including multilingual access and a strategic use of information and communication technologies (ICTs) to build and grow social capital through the creation of hybrid community platforms and ethnic-specific online networks that can address both settlement and more importantly cultural adaptation needs (Hsiao & Dillahunt, 2018). Whatever the inclusion strategy employed their aim must be to foster reciprocity within immigrant communities whilst at the same time trying to reduce uncertainty and build trust when interacting and connecting with local-born inhabitants, with an emphasis on the involvement of trustworthy institutions that are able to facilitate safe resource exchanges and social matching between those immigrant entrepreneurs and established local business networks. Going beyond programme-level interventions, systemic change is required to create a set of truly inclusive digital entrepreneurship ecosystems. This includes the implementation of systemic gender-based analysis in all digital and entrepreneurship policies and programmes to seek to identify and address unintended biases (Orser et al., 2019; Kalkanci et al., 2019). The collation and publication of disaggregated data on programmatic participation and resulting outcomes across demographic dimensions would increase transparency and foster accountability for inclusion (Rowe, 2016). The development of procurement policies that can stimulate opportunities for diverse DSE, potentially including set-asides, positive discrimination or preferences for disadvantaged entrepreneurs can subsequently create market opportunities that support inclusive growth (Loosemore, 2015). Finally, the fostering of coordination between diverse support organisations can create a more coherent pathway for disadvantaged entrepreneurs, by reducing the navigational burden that is often the thing that prevents these entrepreneurs from being able to access all the relevant available resources that are potentially available to them.

Technological Capabilities for different Scaling Strategies

Each form of scaling strategy necessitates its own taxonomy of technological capabilities and the DSE must consider which approach is best suited to its own individual circumstances, ambitions and environment and from these which areas should focus be placed on in order to support growth. Having an understanding of these relationships is a crucial factor for making the necessary strategic technology decisions that are appropriate, and which align properly with scaling objectives. If scaling out is the chosen strategy, then technological capabilities that support substantial and rapid growth of users and geographical reach is required. Appropriate network effect mechanisms have to be built into a platform's architecture to create the self-reinforcing growth cycles that can accelerate user acquisition and engagement (Parker et al., 2016). Technologies which offer benefits around language translation and cultural interpretation will be particularly important for the DSE looking to scale whilst remaining inclusive (Luo & Shenkar, 2017). Issues around currency exchange and local practice can also be addressed with appropriate technology allowing the DSE to operate effectively in an international context whilst maintaining consistency and not compromising the brand. When scaling up is the chosen strategy it requires technologies that support the growth of ecosystems and the building of institutional change (Isenberg & Onyemah, 2016). The development of open-source frameworks can enable other DSEs to build upon and adapt appropriate technologies which can have a multiplying effect and impact beyond what any single organisation could achieve on their own (Bhatt et al., 2016). The use of data sharing and analytical capabilities can further enable organisations to generate insights that can in turn be utilised to inform policy advocacy and further demonstrate societal impact to institutional stakeholders (Tadi, 2021). organisations adopting a scaling up strategy will be well placed for greater information sharing and collaboration and distributed ledger technologies have the potential to allow complex organisations to work closely with others without raising issues around trust and control. However, these technologies can also introduce greater complexity and can then create new barriers for organisations with limited technical capacity. When considering scaling deep, technologies are required that support the building of relationships, learning, and evoke cultural transformation (Riddell & Moore, 2015). Community building platforms have to facilitate meaningful interactions between users and relationship formation instead of more traditional information exchanges. This necessitates the use of sophisticated approaches to both community governance and conflict resolution (Ansell & Gash, 2018). Slingerland et al. (2023) highlight the important role played by storytelling and shared narratives as a means of transferring valuable knowledge, experience, and disseminating lessons learned. The integration of time spent both offline and online becomes particularly important for scaling deep, as creating a lasting cultural change can often require the combination of digital convenience with face-to-face relationship building (Townsend et al., 2016). Technologies that can help to support hybrid events, local chapter organisation and community-led initiatives can aid organisations in fostering and maintaining depth whilst simultaneously achieving greater reach (Christens & Inzeo, 2015). However, these hybrid approaches do require careful design to help avoid favouring either online or offline participants. Learning management and knowledge sharing systems can be used to support the educational and capacity-building activities that are known to be central to scaling deep (An et al., 2014). Technologies which adapt to the specific needs of the learning are also important in terms of digital inclusivity as they respond directly to the user (Isaeva et al., 2025).

Technology Development Approaches and Inclusion

The approaches that DSEs utilise for their technology development significantly influence their ability to create both inclusive solutions and scale equitably (Rengaraju et al., 2024). The variation of development methodologies and practices can have the effect of either reinforcing existing inequalities or actively promoting inclusion and empowerment. Open-source technologies clearly bring opportunities for disadvantaged users as they reduce barriers to uptake and allow customisation of tools to suit the specific needs of the user whilst also keeping costs down (von Hippel & von Krogh, 2003). Open-source initiatives undoubtedly make technology more accessible to the DSE (Maxwell, 2006). However, open-source development can also necessitate a significant technical capacity and community management skills that may not be readily available to all DSEs. The governance of these open-source projects can sometimes reproduce existing power dynamics if any barriers to participation are not actively addressed. Participatory design methodologies aim to involve the intended users in the design process from the earliest possible stages. This seeks to ensure that where digital tools are employed, they fulfil a clear organisational need (Bratteteig & Wagner, 2016). For disadvantaged users this is particularly important as this reduces the risk of bias or the imposition of well-intentioned but inappropriate solutions on the organisation (Offenheiser et al., 2003). Agile and flexible digital solutions offer the greatest benefit to the DSE seeking to promote inclusivity and this needs (to) to be taken into account during the design phase (Özman & Gossart, 2024). This has particular significance for disadvantaged populations as it is possible to tailor solutions to the individual however some consideration is needed around the type of support this requires, and the associated time commitment involved. Furthermore, in order to build a sustainable solution, the support of the community and other key stakeholders is required (Wenger et al., 2009). Approaches which address these issues through the development of local community champions who can offer solutions at a local level through peer-to-peer support have been shown to work well with communities which are disadvantaged. Such interventions where the community takes ownership of the problem (Bakardjieva & Feenberg, 2002). and subsequent solutions ensure technologies used remain relevant and tailored to the needs of the individuals on the ground (Roco, 2008). Care should also be taken to ensure that bureaucracy around community owned resources does not get in the way of these solutions (Zerbe, 2005).

Ethical Considerations in Technological Scaling

As DSEs grow their digital capabilities the ethical considerations also grow and the challenge of facilitating sustainable growth of the organisation without compromising the organisations social aim also becomes more complex in nature (Urmanaviciene & Barasa, 2024). These ethical challenges become increasingly complex as organisations start to operate across increasingly diverse contexts with growing variances in cultural norms, legal frameworks, and power structures that have to be navigated (Urmanaviciene & Barasa, 2024). The challenges that are presented by privacy and data ethics are fundamental for DSEs, in particular for those serving vulnerable populations who may be at risk of surveillance, any form of discrimination or exploitation based on their data (Vayena & Tasioulas, 2016). Stringent data protection processes and systems are needed to maintain a consistent approach in today's global and diverse digital marketplace (Mbah, 2024). The areas of informed consent and agency become particularly complex when working with disadvantaged populations who in themselves may have limited understanding of technological systems or can even feel pressured to participate because of their vulnerable circumstances (Aldridge, 2014). There is a need therefore for organisations to develop approaches to enable informed consent that account for widely varying literacy levels, numerous cultural contexts and power dynamics (Bhutta, 2004). Tensions may be experienced between the ethical principles of the DSE and the effects of algorithm driven technologies (Noble, 2018). As a result, it is vital that DSEs conduct regular digital monitoring to ensure they remain vigilant to unintended bias and are retaining the principles of inclusivity at all levels (Wang et al., 2024). In this way it will be possible to ensure that algorithms, where used, are not undermining the values and ethos of the organisation (Fanni et al., 2023). Increasing digital dependency and rising platform power raises questions about the long-term sustainability and autonomy of communities that can become over-reliant on specific technological platforms or services (Gümüsay et al., 2020). Organisations must consider how their scaling strategies affect communities' ability to undertake self-determination and whether their technologies enhance or reduce the local capacity for independent problem-solving and it is important that practices and processes are designed to align digital practices with culture and empower communities (O'Neill, 2022). What can at first appear to be a neutral technological solution may actually have profound cultural implications when implemented in different contexts (Sun, 2012). Organisations must develop cultural competency and work with local partners to ensure that their technologies support rather than undermine community values and social cohesion (Zinnbauer, 2007). Environmental sustainability considerations become increasingly relevant as DSEs scale, given the significant energy consumption and environmental impact of a growing digital infrastructure (UNDP, 2020). Technology offers huge potential benefits for the DSE however there is also a potential environmental cost of embracing technology which are likely to be at odds with the social aim of the DSE. This can be expressed in a variety of terms such as carbon footprint and energy consumption however to address these traditional approaches to minimise the negative environmental impact of technology uptake can be used in conjunction with approaches which maximise the environmental impact of the organisation. In this way technologies can be selected which bring additional environmental benefits (Ayoungman et al., 2023).

Future Directions and Emerging Technologies

There are a number of important trends relating to technology which have the potential to shape the future of business. Artificial intelligence and machine learning will be a key driver across all contexts (Shepherd & Majchrzak, 2022) and AI technologies offer capabilities hitherto undreamed of (O'Neil, 2017). Traditionally AI was perceived as a privileged technology which few could access or understand however more recently this has become democratised by the release of AI driven tools which are free at the point of delivery (Sundberg & Holmström, 2023). The importance, however, is developed around the principle of inclusivity cannot be overstated here. Another important driver is the rise of technologies which support the decentralisation of information and capital. This alongside the growth in peer supported online learning will create real opportunities for the DSE (Anthony Jnr, 2023) by placing the individual at the centre of things and placing their destiny to some extent in their own hands (Larios-Hernández, 2017) enabling them to identify and act on appropriate economic opportunities (Osho, 2024). Again, however, effort must be made to ensure that individuals are not excluded from this opportunity on the grounds of issues such as digital poverty or lack of other resources (Al-Saqaf & Seidler, 2017). The growth of the Internet of Things (IoT) will also bring benefits for the DSE as technology becomes more widespread, user friendly and inclusive (Haller et al., 2008). Other technologies which provide real time data and which support quick decision making will also continue to be important to the DSE (Singh & Nayyar, 2024). Virtual and augmented reality is becoming more widely utilised but their mainstream potential for providing connected and immersive experiences has still largely been untapped (Yadav, 2025). However, as uptake of these technologies grows, their complexity reduces and the cost of the technology becomes more affordable this potential will be realised more and more (Guo et al., 2025). To support these developments, it is hoped that limitations around digital infrastructure will be addressed (Djatmiko et al., 2025) and that greater connectivity is achieved for all users which overcomes limitations around connectivity and broadband speeds which currently limit digital uptake in disadvantaged groups and communities (Salman et al., 2015). These improvements in digital infrastructure are essential for economic growth (Yetti, 2024) and if introduced in conjunction with digital skills interventions then this could have a tremendous effect on the digital capability of the DSE (Taylor, 2021). AI-powered technologies which deliver personalisation (Rizvi, 2023) and local orientation will also be critical to the DSE (George and George, 2024).

Case Studies of Inclusive Digital Social Entrepreneurship

To provide an illustration of how these principles can be applied in practice, case studies are a useful source to highlight real world initiatives that are currently effectively addressing inclusivity challenges in DSE as these can demonstrate the various approaches being utilised to overcome barriers and create opportunities for disadvantaged entrepreneurs. Laboratoria is an example that offers a comprehensive approach to addressing the issue of gender gaps in the digital economy. With bases of operations across several Latin American countries, this is a social enterprise that selects women from low-income backgrounds that have very limited access to quality higher education. It then provides them with an intensive six-month training program in web development and user experience design. Beyond these technical skills, Laboratoria also focuses on building personal confidence, developing professional networks and workplace skills that are deemed essential for success in technology focused careers. This applies an innovative model whereby alumni make a contribution to the cost of the programme once they have found a technology job in industry (Martínez-Restrepo & Gray, 2020). This system and other similar financing models have the potential to address a number of forms of disadvantage such as gender and income inequality. In this specific case this approach has delivered high rates of graduate employment with 70% of alumni securing quality employment in the digital sector. This illustrates how appropriate interventions can target and overcome a range of barriers. In the case of Kiva which has been designed with inclusivity and accessibility at its heart, this platform provides access to a global marketplace to individuals and groups that previously could not have hoped to be part of. It serves as a crowdfunding platform connecting a number of potential lenders with entrepreneurs worldwide, allowing Kiva to pioneer an approach to make digital financial services accessible to disadvantaged entrepreneurs through developing innovative strategies. Kiva works with local field partners whose role is to provide in-person support to entrepreneurs with limited digital literacy, allowing the gap between global digital networks and local contexts to be bridged. They have developed simplified mobile interfaces that have full functionality on even the most basic smartphones, recognising the likelihood that many of their potential borrowers may have limited access to more advanced devices. Kiva builds trust through the use of community-based systems of verification rather than more traditional credit scoring, which will often be disadvantageous to marginalised entrepreneurs who often lack formal credit scoring histories. Additionally, Kiva's platform provides multilingual support and aims to generate culturally sensitive user communications to accommodate their diverse client portfolio (Braund & Schwittay, 2016). Their approach to inclusive digital innovation demonstrates how technology can be readily adapted and supplemented to help reach more disadvantaged entrepreneurs while simultaneously leveraging the efficiency and reach of digital platforms. By 2023 Kiva was operating in 77 countries globally, had extended loans of $1.7 billion and 80% of its 4 million strong borrowing community were female. Digital Pathways India is an excellent illustration of a systemic approach to digital inclusion that aims to address potential structural barriers rather than placing the focus solely on individual entrepreneurs. This initiative employs a combination of policy advocacy, technology development and capacity building to develop and create an inclusive digital ecosystem through the use of multiple coordinated interventions. Initiatives aimed at reducing barriers to entry for DSEs in the form of affordable or free access to digital tools or tailored support for smaller businesses which lack the resources of their larger competitors can significantly improve digital uptake. In addition this builds links between formal and informal economies through the use of appropriate digital interfaces that enables informal entrepreneurs to access more formal markets without the requirement of undertaking complete formalisation (Acquah et al., 2024). This systemic approach seeks to recognise that inclusivity requires coordinated interventions across a number of dimensions of the broader entrepreneurship ecosystem. This has implications not only for the individual but for the structural factors that determine who is able to access digital support interventions and who is not.

Conclusion

Looking to the future there is a compelling need to develop effective and integrated digital and physical ecosystems which are capable of capitalising fully on the huge opportunities which these existing and emerging technologies present (Yáñez-Valdés et al., 2023). Research shows that effective scaling generally involves synthesising both the physical and the digital in order to leverage the benefits offered by both approaches (Özman & Gossart, 2024). This hybrid approach has the potential to sustainable support growth without compromising the social aim of the organisation (Ravishankar, 2021; Muthukrishnan & Bhattacharyya, 2024). Where communities experience issues around inclusivity hubs which provide access to both physical and digital support services will have the greatest chance of success (Son & Niehm, 2021). All of these models recognise that to have truly inclusive digital social entrepreneurship it must form a bridge between the digital and physical worlds rather than treating them as two separate domains. Policy and regulatory frameworks will need to evolve to support inclusive digital social entrepreneurship while addressing the risks and challenges that emerge as these technologies scale (Usman et al., 2024). Procurement policies are also needed which are sympathetic to issues around privacy and inclusivity (Djatmiko et al., 2025). In the ever evolving digital world of business collaboration and information transfer will more and more become the norm for the DSE (Radanliev, 2025) and the digital social entrepreneur needs to give some thought on the best approaches to sharing and collaborating in a digital sense with stakeholders (Juusola et al., 2024) in order to maximise their social impact (George & George, 2024).

This analysis has demonstrated that digital technologies are not merely tools that can be added to existing social entrepreneurship approaches; rather they can fundamentally transform how social value is created, co-created, delivered, and then scaled, which will require new frameworks for building our understanding and implementing social innovation in the future. The three scaling strategies - scaling out, scaling up, and scaling deep - each interact in different ways with digital technologies. When considering scaling strategies, it is important to remember that digital technologies have the power to connect or isolate. Scaling up offers benefits around knowledge sharing but brings challenges around digital knowledge and the centralisation of power. Scaling deep supports the development of digitally connected communities and sharing of knowledge through networks, but issues around digital isolation may still be noted. Unsurprisingly the greatest potential benefit may come from the adoption of hybrid scaling strategies which incorporate elements of each approach which are selected for their appropriateness to the organisation itself. To support this a holistic and integrated approach is needed whereby policy and practice are closely aligned in order to maximise the impact of scaling activities and ensure inclusivity. The associated technological implications of scaling reveal that the infrastructure choices made early on in an organisation's development have lasting consequences for both scaling potential and inclusivity outcomes. The implementation of different scaling strategies requires distinct technological capabilities and the approaches taken to technology development can significantly influence whether the solutions that are developed serve or exclude disadvantaged populations. Unsurprisingly ethical considerations become increasingly complex as organisations continue to scale across diverse contexts, requiring careful attention to be paid to privacy, algorithmic justice, community autonomy, and cultural integrity. Looking to the future, the important role which will be played by emerging technologies cannot be ignored. The potential offered by artificial intelligence, virtual, augmented, and mixed reality and distributed ledger technologies as examples seems limitless. These create new opportunities for DSEs but also challenges. Embedding digital technologies in the business model requires investment and an ongoing commitment to training and the alignment of social principles and ethical requirements to ensure the benefits of technology uptake are enjoyed by everyone and not just the privileged few. What does seem apparent is that in order to build networks and trust in the marketplace the adoption of hybrid models should be considered by the social enterprise which are not solely focussed on digital strategies, but which combine digital approaches with face-to-face approaches aimed at leveraging the types of relationships which social enterprise tend to be able to develop effectively. Creating such hybrid models often requires coordination across multiple stakeholders' groups and organisational scales, which moves beyond the individual organisations efforts to collectively build ecosystems that support the inclusive digital social innovation agenda. Ultimately, the huge transformative potential of DSE can only be realised if society collectively commits to the practice of centring values of inclusion, justice and human dignity in our future technological choices and implementations. This requires a holistic approach whereby stakeholders work together in order to ensure that digital development, uptake, and capability takes place appropriately and in an inclusive manner for the benefit of all rather than for the sake of technological advancement. In this way the DSE can position itself at the heart of communities not just locally, but regionally, nationally and internationally (Box 5.1). The frameworks and insights presented here aim to provide a foundation for this critical work, however, ultimately their value will very much depend on how they are applied in practice to create future digital social innovations that truly serve all members of our global community.

Box 5.1 Practical Insights Scaling Digital Social Enterprises: Technological Challenges and Solution Strategies

Darin Bifani

Digital Social Enterprises (DSEs) have unprecedented growth and impact opportunities. Despite the opportunity to effect change on a global scale, DSEs often face technological challenges when scaling their businesses, including identifying appropriate technological resources, selecting tools that fit their business model and corporate DNA, and implementing and maintaining a well-designed technological plan. These are complex and often multi-faceted challenges, especially for DSEs with limited technological know-how and time to spend navigating technological issues. After discussing how technology can drive DSE growth, this chapter of the book sets forth technological challenges that DSEs face when scaling and outlines a practical approach that DSEs can use to overcome them.

Unprecedented DSE Scaling Opportunities

For several reasons, DSEs have unprecedented opportunities to bring about social change.

Lean launch models. Unlike traditional brick-and-mortar businesses, DSEs can often be launched with relatively few resources. This has dramatically reduced market entry barriers and operating costs and significantly altered the resources a DSE requires to generate impact. As digital market interconnectivity has exponentially grown, fewer and fewer resources are needed to create the same or larger amounts of social impact. This fundamental change in the relationship between required resources and potential impact gives DSEs an unprecedented opportunity to make significant strides in addressing social problems that historically have required resources that DSEs often did not have.

Digital resource access. DSEs have instant access to massive amounts of digital resources, including information, tools, and massive and often interconnected online communities, all key factors of DSE scaling potential, pathways, and speed. Instant access to deep digital resources can help DSEs deeply understand targeted problems, study real-world examples of what has worked, and create data-supported action steps. In many cases, DSEs can obtain these resources for free.

For example, a DSE focused on improving rural education outcomes in poor areas in India could use free YouTube tutorials to train volunteer educators in small villages, dramatically reducing training costs and raising education levels.

Adoption potential and business model iteration. Regardless of how innovative its business model is and its potential, a DSE's impact is ultimately a function of user adoption of a DSE vision, approach, or service. DSEs can instantly connect with massive numbers of end-user targets in every corner of the globe, significantly increasing impact potential.

Apart from degrees and duration of service adoption, direct and real-time connections with a massive target audience allow DSEs to get wide and up-to-date perspectives on end-user needs and challenges, strengthen DSE strategy, prioritise scaling steps, and design and implement effective scaling pathways. Direct connection with a target audience can significantly shorten the DSE impact cycle, comprising the period from original DSE idea conception to measurable impact, saving costs and allowing additional resources to be used to implement the DSE's impact vision. This creates a virtuous DSE impact cycle, where cycle efficiencies can be reinvested to generate further impact cycle efficiencies.

Improving cost/impact ratios and shrinking DSE impact cycles also significantly increase positive business model iteration opportunities. For traditional brick-and-mortar businesses, rolling out a new business often takes a great deal of time and resources, and if there is a product and demand mismatch, it can take a long time for businesses to pivot, reset their strategic objectives, align necessary resources, and relaunch. Long iteration business cycles create the risks of companies being a crucial step behind market realities and demand, increasing the likelihood of further market mismatches when products or services are relaunched. On the other hand, DSEs, due to lighter infrastructure and lower resource requirements, can often pivot faster, giving them a greater ability to test different business models, iterate faster towards stronger market and product fit matches, and increase the overall probability of social enterprise success.

Growth Potential in the Age of Digital Assets

Scaling any business, including a DSE, presents many strategic and practical challenges. Technology can play a significant role in increasing the chances of scaling success and reducing scaling risk.

Assets in the digital age. We live in an age where the relationship between a business and the assets it can use to grow has fundamentally changed. For a large portion of business history, the issue of what constitutes a company's assets has been defined within a relatively narrow set of corporate and legal parameters. Historically, people have considered business assets to be items that a company owns and can be listed on a company's balance sheet. In this view of assets, there is a clear divide between the assets a company can access and use to drive its business model and assets external to its business that it cannot.

Yet, as we continue to advance further and further in the digital age, the concept of assets has taken on a much broader meaning and practical significance. Every free digital tool, including information, different types of applications, and even entire open-source platforms, is an asset that a firm can use to build its business. This requires a fundamental mental and practical shift in how we view and use potential tools that can be used to scale any business, including a DSE. In many senses, for the first time in history, we are at a point where the potentially most powerful assets of a business are not owned by the company at all.

Even concerning digital assets that are not free, such as software that is licensed under a SaaS model, these assets often can be used based on fractionalised economic terms, often generating significant value creation upside at a usually limited cost that can be terminated if the software does not create expected value. With business models that are based on asset purchases, economically underperforming assets can be challenging to replace, creating a drag on business operating efficiency and growth potential for at times years.

AI as a rising technological intermediary. Coupled with digital asset availability is markedly increased digital asset adoption possibility. Previously, analysing and using types of digital assets often required technical skills that many DSEs, particularly those at an early stage of operations, did not have. Due to limited firm technological comfort levels, this led to situations where technological tools were not adopted, even though they could dramatically improve business performance. *However, with the advent of technology such as AI, which is not only a technological tool but can also show people how to use technology, it is possible to dramatically alter the technology adoption curve.*

As AI can now serve as a technological intermediary that can bridge the gap between technological know-how and technological tool availability, people with limited technical skill sets can implement technology that previously could have only been evaluated and implemented by experts. For example, an agriculture sector-focused DSE in Chile could use ChatGPT to help a non-technical founder set up automated workflows using tools like Notion, allowing the DSE to manage projects, streamline workflows, and drive community engagement without hiring a dedicated IT professional or a full-time IT staff.

The availability of low-cost technical intermediation frees many entrepreneurs from what has historically been the large trap of being forced to operate within the confines of limited technological experience and capability. While technological intermediation cannot eliminate all technology and technological competence gaps, it can reduce those gaps dramatically.

Technological Scaling Pathways

Digital assets, of course, include technology. There are several key ways that technology can help companies scale.

Business plan development. DSEs, like all businesses, must start their social initiative efforts with a deep understanding of the problem to be addressed, develop a vision for addressing that problem, and then design a comprehensive plan to help reduce or eliminate it.

The strength and viability of each of these components of the DSE fundamental strategy are heavily dependent on data. If a DSE's strategy is built on an erroneous view of the market, the needs of its target audience, or reasons why previous efforts to address the issue have not been successful, its efforts are highly likely to fail. Similarly, even if a DSE starts with a good idea, the market may shift during the business implementation phase, which can significantly reduce the strategy's effectiveness.

Conversely, if a DSE develops a correct strategy based on good data, the chances for success dramatically increase. Technology, such as AI, is a potent tool for gathering large amounts of data related to the target problem or audience, analysing it, and using it to drive strategy. AI and other technological tools can be used to continually build and reanalyse data that is relevant for a DSE, allowing it to improve its strategy as it deploys its business model.

For example, a DSE trying to reduce food shortages or insecurity in Latin America could use AI-powered technology to analyse social media posts and other information sources about hunger, which could help it to identify underserved regions, gain a deeper understanding of economic and social hunger drivers and, based on this understanding, create a more effective hunger reduction strategy.

Resource acquisition. A second element of scaling a DSE is acquiring resources, including internal and external human resources. Technology is a very powerful tool that can be used to help DSEs identify and obtain the resources that they need to grow.

To take one example, on many occasions, the process of finding persons for positions is highly inefficient because positions are not correctly defined, and the candidate search process is overly limited. However, by using technology, the process of finding and onboarding human resources can be made considerably more efficient by:

- mapping human resources needs to drive strategy based on DSE objectives, as well as the DSE's unique organisational structure;
- creating detailed profiles of requirements to facilitate the human resource search;
- designing compensation packages with KPIs to drive organisational objectives; and
- creating a comprehensive onboarding plan.

For example, a DSE in France building mental health support communities could use technology to create a digital matching platform to source skilled volunteer counselors in different parts of France. The platform could ensure better alignment between volunteers and user needs by integrating technology-driven personality and skills assessments into the interview, onboarding, and training processes.

One specific type of resource that DSEs often need is capital. Similar to the search for human resources, searches for capital are often highly inefficient and unfortunately often result in pitching the wrong investment propositions to the wrong investors. While there is always uncertainty in the capital raising process, with technology, this process can be made considerably more efficient and increase the chances of raising needed capital on fair terms.

Technology can assist the process by screening for potential investors, matching pitches with investor profiles, and basing targeted investment terms and conditions on the company's specific situation and prevailing market realities.

Operation scaling. One of the most challenging parts of DSE scaling is growing its operational infrastructure. This is difficult because it often requires a significant change in how people relate to each other and how work is done.

When a relatively small DSE and core team members know each other well, operational dynamics are easier to manage. However, as the firm gets larger, organisational dynamics become more complicated, forms of communication become spread out and the amount of information in the firm increases, often exponentially. As this occurs, the very firm dynamics that helped a DSE gain initial traction may become obstacles once the firm passes a certain size threshold. A strong and well-thought-out framework is required to preserve the firm's core strengths, direct firm action, and help management understand as quickly as possible when the firm is veering from its strategic objective.

Technology can play a strong role in supporting this process by:

- Creating operating platforms that permit team members to interact, collaborate, and make efficient business-related decisions;
- Creating cross-functional or cross-departmental platforms that allow relevant information to be stored; and
- Creating CRM platforms that allow companies to efficiently interact with clients or target offices and process feedback from the interactions that can be used to drive service delivery and system improvements.

Drive marketing initiatives and audience engagement. Marketing is also vital for scaling. For people to adopt DSE solutions, they must be aware that the services exist. This is a difficult challenge in a crowded digital world, as many competing demands on user attention and time exist. A technology-driven approach can help define and prioritise target market audience profiles, reach out to that audience continuously, and analyse what marketing messages generate the most audience engagement.

For example, a DSE offering telehealth services in Vietnam could use targeted social media campaigns using AI-generated copy and A/B testing, which could accelerate outreach efforts and boost new user registration.

Driving inclusivity objectives. Another area where technology can help companies scale is by driving inclusivity objectives. Inclusiveness strategies can be beneficial for DSEs, as they can help identify talent in underrepresented groups or in underrepresented regions. Apart from identifying talent for particular positions, this can also give DSE's unique perspective regarding market needs and product or service market fit. An example of this is the African company Andela, which uses AI to identify software talent in Africa and connect that talent with global software companies. Andela's business model helps overcome location biases with coding tests that are not dependent on a specific geographical area. Identifying talent in underrepresented groups and areas can be challenging because people in these groups may have non-traditional career paths or may fall outside the traditional recruiting and networking channels.

Here, technology can be useful for conducting broader searches for potential candidates in multiple languages across multiple channels. An example of a company that employs an inclusive outreach strategy includes HireVue, which uses technology such as Whatsapp and SMS to engage with potential interviewees.

Apart from searching for potential candidates, technology can be used to support the recruiting process by designing appropriate compensation packages and employment terms. An example of a company that uses technology to address this issue is Payscale, which allows companies to design local-adjusted, equitable compensation packages that account for local purchasing power and norms.

Additionally, technology can be used to smooth the onboarding and operating process going forward. An example of this is GitLab, which created an entire onboarding framework using internal wikis, asynchronous communication and AI-guided documentation.
Technology can also be used to help rethink feedback on work so employees can have a clear pathway forward for growth in a company, helping the DSE to retain valuable employees. An example of this is Plum,io, which uses AI to identify individual employee strengths and align them with career pathways, often used by mission driven firms to retain diverse talent.

Inclusivity Objective	*Technology Enabler*	*Inclusivity Impact*
Identifying diverse talent	AI-supported talent matching, geographically-blind skills testing	Find hidden talent in overlooked communities or in candidate pools with non-traditional backgrounds
Reaching underserved candidates and non-traditional candidate groups	Chatbots, SMS outreach, local language applications	Breaks language, digital, and social barriers
Designing fair compensation packages	Global salary benchmarks, benefit structuring, compensation adjustments, contract automation	Ensures fairness across diverse regions while allowing companies to attract the talent they need to be successful and grow
Driving onboarding and remote enablement	Digital learning data bases, interactive digital learning tools, AI-supporting coaching	Accelerating onboarding transitions, helping employees do their jobs more effectively, strengthening service deliver
Providing feedback and supporting career growth	AI-based feedback systems, skill-matching tools, dynamically designing career growth paths	Helps retain talent through clear growth pathways

DSE Scaling Challenges

Despite this opportunity and the power of technologically-driven scaling pathways, scaling DSEs face many scaling challenges. Some of these challenges are similar to the scaling of any business, including having an appropriate business plan and having the resources to execute that plan.

DSEs often face numerous technological challenges as they try to scale.

Lack of knowledge of available digital assets. One of the first challenges that DSEs face is simply understanding what digital assets exist and how those assets can be used to solve different DSE scaling issues at different points in time. Without this knowledge, digital assets cannot be appropriately evaluated.

This is a significant problem because many thousands of possible solutions can be applied to different problems. As few companies have the resources to analyse potential solutions exhaustively, different organisational and other dynamics may lead companies to only consider a few technological options, which may not be the best for a company.

Technology mismatches. A second technological challenge related to scaling is matching a proposed technological solution with the company's problems. Key types of mismatches that can occur are:

- the technology does not solve the core challenge that a DSE is facing;
- the technology is too difficult for a company to implement given its technological know-how, its organisational structure or organisational dynamics;
- the technology cannot be implemented quickly enough;
- the technology is too expensive for the company's budget or considering expected technological benefits; and
- the company will likely outgrow the technological solution quickly, requiring a large expenditure of resources to upgrade to a new technological solution.

Technology implementation. A third challenge is implementing specific technological solutions. Different companies have different types of DNA, with some companies more technically inclined than others. Suppose a company with a low technological DNA tries to implement highly complicated technological tools. In that case, there is a good chance that the tools will not be implemented well and may end up hurting the DSE's growth trajectory rather than helping it.

Technology plan drift. A fourth challenge is revising the company's digital assets as it grows to improve its focus continually. Even in the best of circumstances, technological plans are launched amid highly dynamic situations. Internal and external conditions may change, which can affect the technological tools' functionality and effectiveness.

Solutions to Support Technological Scaling

There are several steps that DSEs can take to overcome technological challenges in the scaling process.

Create a technology oversight role. The first step that DSEs should take is to create a defined role in the organisation that is responsible for technological matters. This is necessary because addressing technological challenges in the scaling process requires consideration of issues in addition to technology, including how the technology fits in with the company's overall strategic objective, organisational dynamics, and project management. If a dedicated resource is not established to handle these issues, there is a great risk that the plan will not be implemented or that it will take longer than expected at a greater cost.

Several models can be used for this:

- Create a dedicated in-house resource. This involves appointing a single person to oversee the design and implementation of the entire technological plan. While this can be the most effective way to manage technology implementation strategies, because the dedicated person is very familiar with company operations and dynamics, DSEs may not have the funds to retain this resource.
- Use a third-party technological solution. The second possibility is for the DSE to retain a third-party solution. While there can be inefficiencies in using third parties to oversee company technological plan implementation initiatives, because they often lack an understanding of non-technical company factors and dynamics, it can be an alternative to a dedicated in-house resource.
- The third possibility is to create a technology committee, where different people in the firm can participate to discuss and implement proposed technological solutions.

Identify opportunities to incorporate technology. The starting point for facing technological challenges is a clear business vision and an understanding of how technology can drive scaling objectives. The business vision should set forth, in detail, not only business objectives, but also a vision of the requirements to support those objectives (see Table 5.1).

Once the relationship between the goal and the requirements for meeting that goal are clearly understood, the DSE can analyse whether there are gaps that could be filled with technology. This requires careful analysis because there are often differences across an organisation regarding the gaps between objectives and requirements. Some companies, for example, may be able to meet growth objectives with resources or technology at hand, while in other cases, it may be extremely unlikely for a company to meet its objectives without significant additional support.

Table 5.1 Objectives, Challenges, and Needs. Created by the Authors

Objective	*Current Challenge*	*Need*
Hiring new people	Traditional outreach efforts have not produced suitable candidates	Use technology to create engagement with potential employees
Improve firm information systems	Firm information has increased and is not stored in an organised way. Team time is lost trying to find relevant information	Use technology to create a system for storing information so that it can easily be found by all team members
Improve client onboarding	Onboarding process is currently slow, and slows down service adoption	Automate the onboarding process
Address customer issues in real time	It takes too long to answer customer questions and address customer issues, which causes them to migrate to other solutions	Use technology to create an automated platform that can answer customer queries in real time in the language of their choice.

Identify technological tools. Once gaps have been identified and prioritised, the next step for a company is to conduct a search for technological tools that could help reduce the gap. This is a significant challenge because there are a large number of technological tools that vary significantly in terms of:

- Core functionality;
- Complexity:
- Degree of integration with other technological tools; and
- Costs.

Given this, DSEs should set up a dedicated process that allows them to identify tools in the market that could help them reduce the gap between their objectives, challenges, and technological solutions.

Conduct a technology audit. Once a set of technological tools has been identified to fill an identified technological gap, an audit should be carried out to determine what technological tools should be used. The technological audit can consider several different factors, including:

- whether the technology will address the core issue and what impact it is expected to have on overall company performance;
- how difficult it would be to implement the technology given the company's current team and technological architecture. As some technology would also affect the relationship with clients, it can be helpful to discuss proposed technological upgrades with representatives of the target audience and see how it will affect their ability to use a particular product or service;
- how much time it would take to implement the technology; and
- another important factor is what the cost would be.

Create a technology scaling plan. Once an audit has been carried out and technology has been identified and costs have been budgeted, the next step is to create a concrete scaling plan.

Key elements of the scaling plan are:

- identification of person or persons who will be on the scaling team, internal or external;
- create a well-structured and reasonable Gantt chart with key technological deliverables;
- an educational phase where employees, and well as clients, understand the changes that will be coming, ask questions, and prepare for upcoming operational changes; and
- the actual implementation of the technology.

Periodically review and update the technological scaling plan. Another critical component of the technological scaling plan is to audit. DSEs do not operate in static environments; internal resources, the target audience, and external market conditions all may change. This means that a technological plan that was appropriate at one point in time may not be appropriate at another.

Because of this, it is important for DSE's to conduct an audit of their technological plan on at least a quarterly basis to evaluate whether it is as effective as possible or if changes should be made.

Conclusion

This book chapter discussed the great opportunities that DSEs have to scale their businesses due to unprecedented levels of interconnectivity with target audiences and the wide availability of digital assets.

Despite this opportunity, DSEs face many technological challenges when scaling, including creating a technological plan, identifying appropriate technological assets, and implementing and making necessary adjustments to technological plans. While these are significant challenges, DSEs have the greatest chance to face and overcome with a comprehensive scaling plan appropriate for the company's business model, resources, and overall technological DNA. Based on these guiding principles, DSEs can create individualised scaling strategies that can take advantage of scaling opportunities and reduce technology-related scaling risk.

The following are some key practical tips to keep in mind to overcome technological scaling challenges:

- Establish a clear firm function to oversee technology-related matters, The function should have clear responsibilities and reporting lines. This function could be carried out by a single person, committee or outside support.
- Conduct a careful audit of firm operations and identify areas where the use of technology can remove inefficiencies and accelerate firm growth.
- Develop a master technological road map focus on driving key organisational objectives.
- Conduct a search for different types of technology that could assist the firm in addressing technological issues
- Create a framework for auditing technology based on various factors, including functional value, expected efficiency gains, ease of implementation and cost.
- Select technology and create a framework for implementation. The implementation plan should include key milestones and set aside time for any training necessary for people who will use the technological solution.
- There should also be a review period after implementation to make any adjustments necessary in light of business progress, market factors and the availability of tool upgrades or different technological tools.

References

Acquah, A., Agyabeng, A.N. and Mensah, J.K., 2024. Digital transformation and implications for the informal sector of Ghana. In *Informal Economy and Sustainable Development Goals: Ideas, Interventions and Challenges*, edited by A. A. Vinodan, S. Mahalakshmi, S. Rameshkumar (pp. 29–51). Emerald Publishing Limited, Bradford, UK

Al-Saqaf, W. and Seidler, N., 2017. Blockchain technology for social impact: Opportunities and challenges ahead. *Journal of Cyber Policy*, *2*(3), pp. 338–354.

Aldridge, J., 2014. Working with vulnerable groups in social research: Dilemmas by default and design. *Qualitative Research*, *14*(1), pp. 112–130.

Allen, D. and Light, J.S. eds., 2015. *From Voice to Influence: Understanding Citizenship in a Digital Age*. University of Chicago Press.

Ameen, N. and Willis, R., 2016. An investigation of the challenges facing the mobile telecommunications industry in United Arab Emirates from the young consumers' perspective. In *27th European Regional Conference of the International Telecommunications Society (ITS): "The Evolution of the North-South Telecommunications Divide: The Role for Europe"*. Cambridge, United Kingdom, 7th–9th September, https://hdl.handle.net/10419/148655

An, X., Deng, H., Chao, L. and Bai, W., 2014. Knowledge management in supporting collaborative innovation community capacity building. *Journal of Knowledge Management*, *18*(3), pp. 574–590.

Ansell, C. and Gash, A., 2018. Collaborative platforms as a governance strategy. *Journal of Public Administration Research and Theory*, *28*(1), pp. 16–32.

Anthony Jnr, B.., 2023. Distributed ledger and decentralised technology adoption for smart digital transition in collaborative enterprise. *Enterprise Information Systems*, *17*(4), p. 1989494.

Austin, J., Stevenson, H. and Wei-Skillern, J., 2006. Social and commercial entrepreneurship: Same, different, or both?. *Entrepreneurship Theory and Practice*, *30*(1), pp. 1–22.

Ayoungman, F.Z., Shawon, A.H., Ahmed, R.R., Khan, M.K. and Islam, M.S., 2023. Exploring the economic impact of institutional entrepreneurship, social Innovation, and poverty reduction on carbon footprint in BRICS countries: What is the role of social enterprise? *Environmental Science and Pollution Research*, *30*(58), pp. 122791–122807.

Bacq, S. and Janssen, F., 2011. The multiple faces of social entrepreneurship: A review of definitional issues based on geographical and thematic criteria. *Entrepreneurship & Regional Development*, *23*(5–6), pp. 373–403.

Bakardjieva, M. and Feenberg, A., 2002. Community technology and democratic rationalization. *The Information Society*, *18*(3), pp. 181–192.

Bhatt, P., Ahmad, A.J. and Roomi, M.A., 2016. Social innovation with open source software: User engagement and development challenges in India. *Technovation*, *52*, pp. 28–39.

Bhutta, Z.A., 2004. Beyond informed consent. *Bulletin of the World Health Organization*, *82*, pp.771–777.

Bratteteig, T. and Wagner, I., 2016. Unpacking the notion of participation in participatory design. *Computer Supported Cooperative Work (CSCW)*, *25*(6), pp. 425–475.

Braund, P. and Schwittay, A., 2016. Scaling inclusive digital innovation successfully: The case of crowdfunding social enterprises. *Innovation and Development*, *6*(1), pp. 15–29.

Charalabidis, Y., Alexopoulos, C. and Loukis, E., 2016. A taxonomy of open government data research areas and topics. *Journal of Organizational Computing and Electronic Commerce*, *26*(1–2), pp. 41–63.

Christens, B.D. and Inzeo, P.T., 2015. Widening the view: Situating collective impact among frameworks for community-led change. *Community Development*, *46*(4), pp. 420–435.

David, A. and Terstriep, J., 2025. Against all odds–migrant entrepreneurs in entrepreneurial ecosystems with constraints. *Journal of Enterprising Communities: People and Places in the Global E*

Djatmiko, G.H., Sinaga, O. and Pawirosumarto, S., 2025. Digital transformation and social inclusion in public services: A qualitative analysis of e-government adoption for marginalized communities in sustainable governance. *Sustainability*, *17*(7), p. 2908.

Drydakis, N., 2024. Reducing the gender digital divide amongst immigrant entrepreneurs. In *Sustainable Economic Development*, edited by Giorgos Meramveliotakis and Manolis Manioudis (pp. 237–264). Routledge.

Erumi-Esin, R. and Heeks, R., 2015, May. e-business adoption and use among African women-owned SMEs: An analytical study in Nigeria. In *Proceedings of the Seventh International Conference on Information and Communication Technologies and Development* (pp. 1–10).

Fanni, R., Steinkogler, V.E., Zampedri, G. and Pierson, J., 2023. Enhancing human agency through redress in Artificial Intelligence Systems. *AI & society*, *38*(2), pp. 537–547.

Fu, X., Ghauri, P., & Lu, J., 2025. Digital technology and inclusive development during global crisis: Evidence from a randomised experiment in Bangladesh. *Research Policy*, *54*(3), p. 105173.

George, A.S. and George, A.H., 2024. Towards a super smart society 5.0: Opportunities and challenges of Integrating emerging technologies for social innovation. *Partners Universal International Research Journal*, *3*(2), pp. 01–29.

Ghalwash, S., Tolba, A. and Ismail, A., 2017. What motivates social entrepreneurs to start social ventures? An exploratory study in the context of a developing economy. https://urn.kb.se/resolve?urn=urn:nbn:se:mdh:diva-67825

Graham, M., 2011. Time machines and virtual portals: The spatialities of the digital divide. *Progress in development studies*, *11*(3), pp. 211–227.

Gümüsay, A.A., Smets, M. and Morris, T., 2020. "God at work": Engaging central and incompatible institutional logics through elastic hybridity. *Academy of Management Journal*, *63*(1), pp. 124–154.

Guo, C., Zhang, H., Chai, Y., Gao, H. and Lv, R., 2025. The impact of AIGC technology penetration in Fintech on entrepreneurship of small and medium-sized enterprises. *International Review of Financial Analysis*, 104656.

Haller, S., Karnouskos, S. and Schroth, C., 2008, September. The internet of things in an enterprise context. In *Future Internet Symposium*, edited by John Domingue, Dieter Fensel, and Paolo Traverso (pp. 14–28). Berlin, Heidelberg: Springer Berlin Heidelberg.

Hsiao, J.C.Y. and Dillahunt, T.R., 2018. Technology to support immigrant access to social capital and adaptation to a new country. *Proceedings of the ACM on Human-Computer Interaction, 2(CSCW)*, pp. 1–21.

Isaeva, R., Karasartova, N., Dznunusnalieva, K., Mirzoeva, K. and Mokliuk, M., 2025. Enhancing learning effectiveness through adaptive learning platforms and emerging computer technologies in education. *Jurnal Ilmiah Ilmu Terapan Universitas Jambi*, *9*(1), pp. 144–160.

Isenberg, D. and Onyemah, V., 2016. Fostering scale up ecosystems for regional economic growth. In *Global Entrepreneurship Congress*, edited by Philip Auerswald Iqbal Quadir (Vol. 11, No. 1, pp. 71–97). Tagore LLC.

Islam, S.M., 2020. Unintended consequences of scaling social impact through ecosystem growth strategy in social enterprise and social entrepreneurship. *Journal of Business Venturing Insights*, *13*, p. e00159.

Islam, S.M., 2022. Social impact scaling strategies in social enterprises: A systematic review and research agenda. *Australian Journal of Management*, *47*(2), pp. 298–321.

Juusola, K., Venkitachalam, K., Kleber, D. and Popat, A., 2024. Knowledge sharing in open social innovation for sustainable development: Evidence from rural social enterprises. *Journal of Strategy and Management*. https://doi.org/10.1108/JSMA-12-2023-0322

Kalkanci, B., Rahmani, M. and Toktay, L.B., 2019. The role of inclusive innovation in promoting social sustainability. *Production and Operations Management*, *28*(12), pp. 2960–2982.

Khajeheian, D. and Friedrichsen, M., 2017. Innovation inventory as a source of creativity for interactive television. *Digital Transformation in Journalism and News Media: Media Management, Media Convergence and Globalization*, (25) pp. 341–349. https://doi.org/10.1007/978-3-319-27786-8_25.

Kusumaningtyas, N. and Suwarto, D.H., 2015. ICT adoption, skill and use differences among small and medium enterprises managers based on demographic factors. *Procedia-Social and Behavioral Sciences*, *169*, pp. 296–302.

Larios-Hernández, G.J., 2017. Blockchain entrepreneurship opportunity in the practices of the unbanked. *Business Horizons*, *60*(6), pp. 865–874.

Loosemore, M., 2015. Building a new third construction sector through social enterprise. *Construction management and economics*, *33*(9), pp. 724–739.

Luo, Y., & Shenkar, O. (2017). The multinational corporation as a multilingual community: Language and organization in a global context. In *Language in International Business: Developing a Field*, edited by M. Yoko Brannen and T. Mughan (pp. 59–92). Cham: Springer International Publishing.

Mack, E.A., Marie-Pierre, L. and Redican, K., 2017. Entrepreneurs' use of internet and social media applications. *Telecommunications Policy*, *41*(2), pp. 120–139.

Martínez-Restrepo, S. and Gray, L., 2020. *Digital Learning Solutions for Women Entrepreneurs in Tech: The Case of Laboratoria*. Coderise.

Martinez Dy, A., Martin, L. and Marlow, S., 2018. Emancipation through digital entrepreneurship? A critical realist analysis. *Organization*, *25*(5), pp. 585–608.

Maxwell, E., 2006. Open standards, open source, and open innovation: Harnessing the benefits of openness. *Innovations: Technology, Governance, Globalization*, *1*(3), pp. 119–176.

Mbah, G.O., 2024. Data privacy in the era of AI: Navigating regulatory landscapes for global businesses. *International Journal of Science and Research Archive*, *13*(2), 2396–2405.

McGann, M., Blomkamp, E. and Lewis, J.M., 2018. The rise of public sector innovation labs: Experiments in design thinking for policy. *Policy Sciences*, *51*(3), pp. 249–267.

Moore, M.L., Riddell, D. and Vocisano, D., 2015. Scaling out, scaling up, scaling deep*: Strategies of non-profits in advancing systemic social innovation. In *Large Systems Change: An Emerging Field of Transformation and Transitions*, edited by Malcolm McIntosh, Steve Waddell, Sandra Waddock, Sarah Cornell, Domenico Dentoni, Milla McLachlan (58) (pp. 67–84). Routledge.

Muthukrishnan, U. and Bhattacharyya, S.S., 2024. Can women empowerment contribute to sustainable growth–examining the enablers for social enterprise performance of women social entrepreneurs in India. *International Journal of Ethics and Systems*. https://doi.org/10.1108/IJOES-09-2023-0211.

Muzellec, L., Ronteau, S. and Lambkin, M., 2015. Two-sided Internet platforms: A business model lifecycle perspective. *Industrial Marketing Management*, *45*, pp. 139–150.

Nambisan, S., 2017. Digital entrepreneurship: Toward a digital technology perspective of entrepreneurship. *Entrepreneurship Theory and Practice*, *41*(6), pp. 1029–1055.

Noble, S.U., 2018. Algorithms of oppression: How search engines reinforce racism. In *Algorithms of Oppression*. New York University Press. https://doi.org/10.18574/nyu/9781479833641.001.0001.

Offenheiser, R.C. and Holcombe, S.H., 2003. Challenges and opportunities in implementing a rights-based approach to development: An Oxfam America perspective. *Nonprofit and Voluntary Sector Quarterly*, *32*(2), pp. 268–301.

O'Neil, C., 2017. *Weapons of Math Destruction: How Big Data Increases Inequality and Threatens Democracy*. Crown.

O'Neill, E., 2022. Contextual integrity as a general conceptual tool for evaluating technological change. *Philosophy & Technology*, *35*(3), p. 79.

Osho, G.O., 2024. Decentralized autonomous organizations (DAOs): A conceptual model for community-owned banking and financial governance. *International Journal of Advanced Multidisciplinary Research and Studies*, *4*(6), pp. 1812–1828.

Orser, B., Riding, A. and Li, Y., 2019. Technology adoption and gender-inclusive entrepreneurship education and training. *International Journal of Gender and Entrepreneurship*, *11*(3), pp. 273–298.

Özman, M. and Gossart, C., 2024. Scaling in social enterprises: The case of digital social innovations. *Management International= International Management= Gestión Internacional*, *28*(4), pp. 55–67.

Parker, G.G., Van Alstyne, M.W. and Choudary, S.P., 2016. *Platform Revolution: How Networked Markets Are Transforming the Economy and How to Make Them Work for You*. WW Norton & Company.

Pariser, E., 2011. *The Filter Bubble: What the Internet Is Hiding from You*. Penguin UK.

Prodanov, H., 2018. Social entrepreneurship and digital technologies. *Economic Alternatives*, *1*(1), pp. 123–138.

Radanliev, P., 2025. Cyber diplomacy: Defining the opportunities for cybersecurity and risks from Artificial Intelligence, IoT, Blockchains, and Quantum Computing. *Journal of Cyber Security Technology*, *9*(1), pp. 28–78.

Rahman, S.A., Taghizadeh, S.K., Ramayah, T. and Alam, M.M.D., 2017. Technology acceptance among micro-entrepreneurs in marginalized social strata: The case of social innovation in Bangladesh. *Technological Forecasting and Social Change*, *118*, pp. 236–245.

Ravishankar, M.N., 2021. Social innovations and the fight against poverty: An analysis of India's first prosocial P2P lending platform. *Information Systems Journal*, *31*(5), pp. 745–766.

Raybourn, E.M., 2014. A new paradigm for serious games: Transmedia learning for more effective training and education. *Journal of Computational Science*, *5*(3), pp. 471–481.

Rengaraju, N., Sankararaman, G., Vembu, N.R., Indhumathi, D. and Rengarajan, V., 2024. Tech-enabled social innovation: The role of digital platforms in social entrepreneurship. *Acta Scientiae*, 07(1), pp. 618–631.

Riddell, D. and Moore, M.L., 2015. *Scaling Out, Scaling Up, Scaling Deep*. McConnell Foundation. JW McConnell Family Foundation & Tamarack Institute.

Rızvı, M., 2023. Investigating AI-powered tutoring systems that adapt to individual student needs, providing personalized guidance and assessments. *The Eurasia Proceedings of Educational and Social Sciences*, *31*, pp. 67–73.

Roco, M.C., 2008. Possibilities for global governance of converging technologies. *Journal of nanoparticle research*, *10*, pp. 11–29.

Rowe, A., 2016. Designing Equality of Opportunity in National Innovation Systems Moving Towards Gender Conscious Policy, Performance Measurement, and Resource Allocation (Doctoral dissertation).

Sahai, A.K. and Rath, N., 2021. Artificial intelligence and the 4th industrial revolution. In *Artificial Intelligence and Machine Learning in Business Management*, edited by Sandeep Kumar Panda, Vaibhav Mishra, R. Balamurali, Ahmed A. Elngar (pp. 127–143). CRC Press.

Salman, O., Elhajj, I., Kayssi, A. and Chehab, A., 2015, December. Edge computing enabling the internet of things. In *2015 IEEE 2nd World Forum on Internet of Things (WF-IoT)* (pp. 603–608). IEEE. doi: 10.1109/WF-IoT.2015.7389122.

Schot, J. and Steinmueller, W.E., 2018. Three frames for innovation policy: R&D, systems of innovation and transformative change. *Research Policy*, *47*(9), pp. 1554–1567.

Singh, B. and Nayyar, A., 2024. Navigating deep learning models and health monitoring infrastructure financing in smart cities: Review from legal perceptions and future innovations. In Deep Learning in Engineering, Energy and Finance, edited by Vivek S. Sharma, Shubham Mahajan, Anand Nayyar, Amit Kant Pandit, pp. 80–114.

Shepherd, D.A. and Majchrzak, A., 2022. Machines augmenting entrepreneurs: Opportunities (and threats) at the Nexus of artificial intelligence and entrepreneurship. *Journal of Business Venturing*, *37*(4), p. 106227

Slingerland, G., Kooijman, J., Lukosch, S., Comes, T. and Brazier, F., 2023. The power of stories: A framework to orchestrate reflection in urban storytelling to form stronger communities. *Community Development*, *54*(1), pp. 18–37.

Son, J. and Niehm, L.S., 2021. Using social media to navigate changing rural markets: The case of small community retail and service businesses. *Journal of Small Business & Entrepreneurship*, *33*(6), pp. 619–637.

Sun, H., 2012. *Cross-cultural Technology Design: Creating Culture-Sensitive Technology for Local Users*. OUP USA.

Sundberg, L. and Holmström, J., 2023. Democratizing artificial intelligence: How no-code AI can leverage machine learning operations. *Business Horizons*, *66*(6), pp. 777–788.

Suseno, Y. and Abbott, L., 2021. Women entrepreneurs' digital social innovation: Linking gender, entrepreneurship, social innovation and information systems. *Information Systems Journal*, *31*(5), pp. 717–744.

Tadi, V., (2021) Interoperability in action: How regulatory and cultural factors shape data sharing in public-private collaborations. *International Journal of Science and Research*, 10(3), pp. 1993–2004.

Taylor, K., 2021. An analysis of the entrepreneurial institutional ecosystems supporting the development of hybrid organizations: The development of cooperatives in the US. *Journal of Environmental Management*, *286*, p. 112244.

Townsend, L., Wallace, C., Smart, A. and Norman, T., 2016. Building virtual bridges: How rural micro-enterprises develop social capital in online and face-to-face settings. *Sociologia Ruralis*, *56*(1), pp. 29–47.

UNCTAD. (2014). *Empowering Women Entrepreneurs through Technology*. [Online] Available: https://unctad.org/publication/empowering-women-entrepreneurs-through-information-and-communications-technologies

UNDP. (2020). *Human Development Report 2020: The Next Frontier - Human Development and the Anthropocene*. [Online] Available: https://hdr.undp.org/content/human-development-report-2020

United Nations. (2019). *Disability and Development Report: Realizing the Sustainable Development Goals by, for and with Persons with Disabilities*. [Online] Available: https://social.un.org/publications/UN-Flagship-Report-Disability-Final.pdf

Urmanaviciene, A. and Barasa, M.S., 2024. Managing ethical challenges in social enterprises. *Business Ethics and Leadership*, *8*(3), pp. 82–96.

Usman, F.O., Kess-Momoh, A.J., Ibeh, C.V., Elufioye, A.E., Ilojianya, V.I. and Oyeyemi, O.P., 2024. Entrepreneurial innovations and trends: A global review: Examining emerging trends, challenges, and opportunities in the field of entrepreneurship, with a focus on how technology and globalization are shaping new business ventures. *International Journal of Science and Research Archive*, *11*(1), pp. 552–569.

Uvin, P., Jain, P.S. and Brown, L.D., 2000. Think large and act small: Toward a new paradigm for NGO scaling up. *World Development*, *28*(8), pp. 1409–1419.

Vayena, E. and Tasioulas, J., 2016. The dynamics of big data and human rights: The case of scientific research. *Philosophical Transactions of the Royal Society A: Mathematical, Physical and Engineering Sciences*, *374*(2083), p. 20160129.

Hippel, E.V. and Krogh, G.V., 2003. Open source software and the "private-collective" innovation model: Issues for organization science. *Organization Science*, *14*(2), pp. 209–223.

Wang, X., Wu, Y.C., Ji, X. and Fu, H., 2024. Algorithmic discrimination: Examining its types and regulatory measures with emphasis on US legal practices. *Frontiers in Artificial Intelligence*, *7*, p. 1320277.

Wenger, E., White, N. and Smith, J.D., 2009. *Digital Habitats: Stewarding Technology for Communities*. CPsquare

Westley, F. and Antadze, N., 2010. Making a difference: Strategies for scaling social innovation for greater impact. *Innovation Journal*, *15*(2), pp. 1–19.

Westley, F., Antadze, N., Riddell, D.J., Robinson, K. and Geobey, S., 2014. Five configurations for scaling up social innovation: Case examples of nonprofit organizations from Canada. *The Journal of Applied Behavioral Science*, *50*(3), pp. 234–260.

Yadav, S., 2025. Transformative learning With advanced technologies: Harnessing VR and AR for immersive educational experiences. In *Revolutionizing Pedagogy Through Smart Education*, edited by Jorge A. Ruiz-Vanoye and Ocotlán Díaz-Parra (pp. 139–156). IGI Global Scientific Publishing.

Yáñez-Valdés, C., Guerrero, M., Barros-Celume, S. and Ibáñez, M.J., 2023. Winds of change due to global lockdowns: Refreshing digital social entrepreneurship research paradigm. *Technological Forecasting and Social Change*, *190*, p. 122454.

Yetti, E., 2024. Pedagogical innovation and curricular adaptation in enhancing digital literacy: A local wisdom approach for sustainable development in Indonesia context. *Journal of Open Innovation: Technology, Market, and Complexity*, *10*(1), p. 100233.

Zerbe, N., 2005. Biodiversity, ownership, and indigenous knowledge: Exploring legal frameworks for community, farmers, and intellectual property rights in Africa. *Ecological Economics*, *53*(4), pp. 493–506.

Zinnbauer, D., 2007. What can Social Capital and ICT do for Inclusion. *Institute for Prospective Technological Studies (IPTS)–JRC–European Commission EUR*, *22673*, pp. 1–40.

Final Insights

A plethora of different insights emerged from the present book. A mix of theoretical and practical approaches are offered. They fully enriched the originality of the book and provided a diverse perspective of digital social entrepreneurship and its implications for people, planet, and profit.

Digital social entrepreneurship is the new global company technologically oriented that aims to solve social problems. Digital technologies are not mere tools but crucial assets. A' la Schumpeter, digital social entrepreneurship is innovative and generates disruptive changes so as to improve quality life for the global community. People become the main focus of digital social enterprises that fully incorporate "altruistic capitalism", based on a " shared purpose and reciprocal obligations within society moving beyond a profit driven model" (Collier, 2019).

Digital social entrepreneurship is ethically founded, prone to promote inclusiveness and equality.

In this realm, technologies such as artificial intelligence, augmented reality, virtual reality, and among others empower enterprises' competencies to reach their social goals. If Smith counted land, labour and capital as main assets, nowadays, the priorities are changed. People drive business models and technologies replace land and capital is still present.

People have a double role: they trigger enterprises activities but they are also recipients of their activities.

In the book, we consider a different range of people, mainly disadvantaged people such as immigrants, victims of violence, not employed and not educated people and so on from different countries like Africa, Italy, Chile, The United Kingdom and Switzerland.

We are in love with the social enterprising journey of Roberta D'Amore, who thanks to her passion she is empowering women in the vibrant heart of Bamako in Mali and then Ouagadougou, capital of Burkina Faso. She is changing their future for the best. Then moving on to Foreword that presents digital social innovations for deaf people. However, such big change cannot occur if technologies are not embraced. Theo Tzanidis has presented their empowerment towards digital social

DOI: 10.4324/9781003583448-7

enterprises. The business model has to be replicable and scalable so as to make a huge social impact for the global community.

Further, Digital Social entrepreneurship is discussed from an SDG standpoint. An illustrative case studies from the People and Planet First database, highlighting practical applications of the DSE–PPP nexus is argued. Moving on, we also consider immigrant entrepreneurs with Alan Murray and Alan Martin to understand the process of scaling.

We conclude with Darin Bifani who has emphasised that technologies can help companies scale by driving inclusivity objectives. Inclusiveness strategies can be beneficial for DSEs, as they can help identify talent in underrepresented groups or in underrepresented regions, breaking language, digital, and social barriers.

Being socially responsible is the new "must have".

Reference

Collier, P. (2019). *The Future of Capitalism: Facing the New Anxieties*, Allen Lane- Penguin Books, UK.

Index

Pages in *italics* refer to figures, pages in **bold** refer to tables, and pages followed by "n" refer to notes.